MINING CAMPS
AND
GHOST TOWNS

**A HISTORY OF MINING IN ARIZONA AND CALIFORNIA
ALONG THE LOWER COLORADO**

by

FRANK LOVE
Professor of Social Science
Arizona Western College

D0871918

Westernlore Press . . . **1974** . . . **Los Angeles 90041**

Library of Congress Catalog No. 73-86960

ISBN No. 0-87026-031-6

PRINTED IN THE UNITED STATES OF AMERICA BY WESTERNLORE PRESS

To Dottie Mae . . .
my own lucky bonanza

PREFACE

ONE OF THE truly great American historians, Frederick Jackson Turner, once noted that the settlement of the frontier seemed to follow a rather rhythmic pattern. The mountain man came into the wilderness first, hoping to make his fortune trading or trapping furs. He was followed by the miner, who exploited the mineral resources. Cattlemen followed, grazing their herds on the open range. Finally came the farmer, fencing the land and ending the frontier forever.

This book is about the mineral frontier, as it affected one section of the vast American West, the Lower Colorado River Region. Yuma, Arizona was, and still is, the nerve center of the area which straddles the Arizona-California border. The town was its supply center, place for raising hell on pay day, and base for prospecting and mining operations. Some of its mining past is still reflected in its friendly attitudes toward strangers, and its casual way of life.

Many persons assisted me while I was writing this book. My wife, Dottie Mae, risked life and limb on a trail bike traveling to remote mining camps. She spent endless hours typing and indexing. I owe thanks to the Yuma County Historical Society, whose devoted effort to preserve some of our past has resulted in an excellent museum, the Century House, and an invaluable collection of letters, photographs, and other memorabilia. The library at Arizona State University contains much valuable material, and the staff in the Arizona Collection was most helpful. The Department of Library and Archives at the State Capitol in Phoenix permitted me to read originals of the *Arizona Sentinel* and *Yuma Sun* newspapers. I am grateful to the Spe-

--◦◦❈{ vii }❈◦◦--

cial Collections Department at the University of Arizona Library for permitting me to use the *Diary* of Louis J. F. Jaeger, a Yuma area pioneer.

Two of my colleagues at Arizona Western College were most helpful. Professor Larry MacDonald of the English Department was kind enough to read my manuscript and offer a number of useful suggestions. Any errors in grammar or style are my responsibility rather than his. Richard Yates, the librarian at Arizona Western College, suggested many useful sources.

One man, who was dead before I was born, deserves my thanks. He was John Dorrington, the fiery, crusading editor of the *Arizona Sentinel*. Reading his newspaper helped me develop respect and admiration for the miners, prospectors, merchants, and just plain citizens who preceded me in this fascinating part of the West.

—FRANK LOVE,
Arizona Western College, Yuma.

CONTENTS

ILLUSTRATIONS

CHAPTER ONE

MYSTERY MINERS ALONG THE COLORADO

THE BEGINNINGS of mining activity along the Lower Colorado River and its tributaries are shrouded in mystery. The historian, if he is honest, cannot say with any degree of certainty who the first miners were. There is proof that the Spaniards who conquered and governed Mexico knew of the existence of rich mineral deposits in the general area, but there has been no positive evidence that they dug the mysterious "old workings" that have been found in various places.

Spanish interest in the region northwest of Mexico dates to the time of Francisco Coronado. His expedition from Mexico in the Sixteenth Century sought the fabled Seven Cities of Cibola in the Southwest, but found instead mud pueblos. Almost a half century passed before the Espejo Expedition entered Arizona in 1582 and discovered silver in the north central section. Herbert Bolton, the great borderlands historian of the Southwest, was of the impression that the mines were west of Prescott, Arizona, along the Bill Williams River.[1] But it was impractical for the Spaniards to develop the mines at that time, and they were left deserted and forgotten. Precious metals could be obtained more cheaply and with less danger to human life in Northern Mexico.

Silver, literally sheets of it lying on or near the surface, rekindled Spanish interest in the region to the northwest of Mexico. The time was the 17th Century and the strike was made along the present United States border with Mexico, near

[1]Herbert Bolton (ed.), *Spanish Explorations in the Southwest: 1542-1706* (New York: Charles Scribner's Sons, 1930), pp. 186-187.

Nogales. Miners called it "Planchas de Plata" and a mining district was established known as "Real de Arizonac," which is the origin of Arizona's name. The bonanza was almost beyond belief. One chunk of silver weighed 425 pounds!

Such a discovery naturally encouraged further exploration of the region and there is some evidence that the miners met with success. General Charles P. Stone discovered a map in the Mexico City archives during Mexican War days which showed the location of nearly 100 mines worked by the Spaniards in the northern provinces.[2] Stone supposedly made a copy of the map, but its whereabouts is unknown at the present time. If it were available, one might ascertain which of the mines were along the Lower Colorado, and the mystery miners might be identified as Spaniards.

Could the mystery miners of the Colorado have been Spaniards? Chances are that they were not. Several fierce tribes inhabited the region. Missionaries did venture into the area several times, but even the cause of God was advanced with much timidity after the Quechans murdered Father Tomas Garces and his fellow Spaniards in 1781.

But someone was mining along the Colorado before the Americans came! Surface diggings were plainly evident in numerous places. Old pits dotted the Castle Dome area, and many of the miners simply looked for an "old digging" and filed a claim on it. There were traces of an old trail along which the mystery miners carried ore to the Gila River. Some of them even reported an ancient smelter along its banks.

No one knew the age of the diggings. It was clear they dated beyond the immediate past. They were filled with debris, and overgrown with mesquite and palo verde trees. North and west of Castle Dome were similar signs. The Plumosa Mountains and the river valley around Ehrenberg had old diggings.

John Parker, a writer for the *Arizona Republic,* has speculated that the mystery miners were Frenchmen. He based his

[2]William P. Blake, "Mining in Arizona," *Arizona and Its Resources,* Aug. 1899, pp. 55-57.

theory on the fact that the Mohave tribe says that there were Frenchmen along the river in the early 19th Century. Their oral tradition is that a large party of Frenchmen entered the area and discovered the mineral outcroppings.[3]

Is it possible that the mystery miners were French? Historians have no difficulty in placing Frenchmen in the region in the early 19th Century. James O. Pattie, an American mountain man from Kentucky, left an extensive account of his travels in Arizona and California in the 1820s. It relates that Pattie first trapped along the Gila with Frenchmen. When one considers that Frenchmen were the real pioneers in the American fur trade, Parker's conclusion gains credibility.

But if Frenchmen were the mystery miners as Parker believed, why did they abandon their mines? The Mohave tradition is that they were driven out. One of the Frenchmen shot a Mohave woman. When the husband accosted the Frenchman who had killed his wife, he laughed as if to imply that the death of one Indian woman was of no importance to a Frenchman. The Mohave tradition holds that this was too much for the peaceful Mohaves to endure, and they drove all the Frenchmen out.

There are other possible solutions to the mystery. One is that Indians may have been the first to mine along the Colorado. This answer has generally been ruled out by professional historians, who argue that the Indians did not use metal.

But no less an authority on Southwestern mining than William P. Blake accepted this solution. Blake was not a historian, but was recognized as the number one authority on Arizona mining at the turn of the century. Writing in 1899, he stated that "The prehistoric races who occupied. . . Arizona . . . were the earliest miners. Evidences of their work is found in all directions."[4]

If the Indians did not use metals as the historians affirm, was Blake completely wrong? Perhaps he wasn't. The Indians may

[3]John L. Parker, "Lost Legends Plentiful in the State," *The Arizona Republic*, Nov. 12, 1961, p. 14.

[4]Blake, *op. cit.*, pp. 55-57.

A "gopher hole" to bedrock.

—*Frank Love Photo.*

have mined the ore in order to use it for manufacturing body paints. All of the early explorers took note of the fact that Indian tribes painted their bodies in various patterns and colors.

One Spaniard thought they were mining for this purpose three hundred years before Blake claimed they were the first miners. Farfan de los Godos was sent into Arizona in 1598 to attempt to relocate Espejo's mine. He told Juan Velarde, who had been assigned to make a record of the trip, that an Indian had given him a piece of pulverized ore. He asked the native to take him to the place from which the ore came and the Indian agreed. Farfan said that ". . . the said mine . . . was at great height . . . There they found an old shaft, three estados in depth, from which *the Indians extracted the ores for their personal adornment* (Italics by the author), because in this mine there are brown, black, water colored, blue, and green ores . . . The mine had a very large dump."[5]

Farfan's statement does not prove that Indians dug the mines along the Colorado, but it does make it an open possibility. However, one problem does arise from this solution to the mystery. A smelter was discovered near Castle Dome by the first Anglo miners, and no smelter would be needed to crush the ore for paints, only some sort of arrastra

Two other solutions are possible. *Mining and Scientific Press,* an authoritative newspaper of the 19th Century mining industry, stated in 1883 that Mexicans had discovered placers on the Lower Colorado in 1775.[6] If they were correct, the old mines may have been dug by Mexican miners. They may have been driven out or massacred at the time of the 1781 Quechan uprising.

There is one other interesting possibility. There have long been rumors that Jesuit missionaries of the Southwest secretly operated silver mines and forwarded the proceeds from them to their religious order in Europe. Competent historians think that such stories are myth, and suggest that they are contra-

[5]Bolton, *op. cit.,* p. 244.
[6]*Mining and Scientific Press,* Nov. 3, 1883, p. 202.

dicted by the lives of men like Father Eusibio Kino. His travels and evangelizing efforts left little time for operating mines.

Yet the stories persist. Can they have any basis in fact? Probably not; but consider this. The Tombstone *Epitaph* told its readers in 1883 that church records in Magdalena (Mexico) show that missionaries worked the Manzanal Mine near there in the 17th Century until driven off by Apaches.[7] The newspaper was probably repeating hearsay, but until some historian either proves or disproves that such records existed and were correct, there is the slim chance that the Jesuits did operate mines and that this explains the old diggings along the Colorado.

Who were the first miners along the Colorado? Your guess is as good as mine.

[7]*Ibid.*, Oct. 13, 1883, p. 229, quoting from *Tombstone Daily Epitaph*, Sept. 28, 1883.

CHAPTER TWO

THE GILA CITY STORY

THE SANDY FOOTHILLS of the Gila Mountains, one and a half miles west of Dome, Arizona, were the site of the first real gold rush in the Lower Colorado River area. The Gila River, now a dry stream bed, passes close to the foothills and empties into the Colorado a mile or so farther west.

Visitors who go to the trouble of searching out the spot will find very little that resembles the ghost towns they have been led to expect from movies or television. Not a single vintage building remains. Only a mining rig of the 1973 generation occupied the grounds when the author recently inspected them. A "Keep out!" sign warned against intrusion.

Jacob Snively, a Texan who had been Sam Houston's secretary, is often given credit for discovering gold along the Gila. He doesn't really deserve the honor because the true discoverer was Henry Birch, a member of his party. Birch picked up a nugget one day in September 1858, after the party had encamped along the river. His find set others looking for gold, and they found plenty.[1]

Newspaper reports about Gila City are not very useful in trying to trace the beginnings of the gold rush that followed because they are somewhat contradictory. *The New York Daily Times* reported during the winter of 1858 that a rush had begun. "At the date of these advices," stated the *Times*, "about the middle of December—there were over six hundred men at

[1]James M. Barney, "Arizona's Trail of Gold," *The Sheriff*, VIII, No. 2 (Feb. 1949), p. 4.

work with the rudest means of operation, making from four to a hundred and fifty dollars per day to the hand."[2]

But the news wasn't the same in Tubac, New Mexico Territory, where the newspaper was telling its readers that the *Times* report was a "tissue of humbuggery." The weekly paper asserted that "No such number of men . . . has ever been at work on the Gila at one time." Only a few men were there, said the paper, and they were barely clearing expenses.[3]

The Tubac editor may not have been entirely objective in his reporting since his newspaper was an arm of the Sonora Mining and Exploring Company which owned silver mines around Tubac. Chances were good that if stories such as the *Times* was printing about the Gila River mines were believed, miners would desert their employment in Southern Arizona to try their luck placering. His personal interests may have dictated that he try to discourage such developments.

It is not possible to determine how rapidly miners descended on the Gila diggings, but it is certain that a fair-sized town had developed a quarter mile east by 1860. The miners called it Gila City. Tent stores sprang up, stocked with ready-made clothing and other luxuries the miners desired. Gambling dens and bars appeared, to help separate the men from their nuggets and dust. Some merchants were soon considering building permanent structures of adobe to replace the brush lean-tos and tent houses.

Gold was generally found near bedrock along the river banks and in the nearby foothills of the low-lying Gila Mountains. Miners had to dig down twenty feet or so to reach pay dirt. As work progressed on such a "gopher hole," an occasional pan of dirt was tested to ascertain whether it was likely that the search would be successful. Once the digger reached the level where gold was found in paying quantities, the gravel was removed and transported to the riverside for washing or "panning."

[2]*The Weekly Arizonian*, Tubac, A.T., Mar. 3, 1859, quoting the *New York Daily Times*, n.d.
[3]*Ibid.*, Mar. 3, 1859.

Panning wasn't quite as simple as western lore suggests, but it wasn't so difficult that the novice couldn't learn with a little practice. Several inches of gravel was placed in a metal pan and river water introduced. By working the pan in a gentle rolling motion while tossing out large chunks of waste, the sand was slowly washed over the edges. Hopefully, tiny flakes of gold which were heavier than the other materials would remain. Dust gathered in this manner was carefully stored in a can or bottle. One Gila City miner who managed to collect a can of the precious metal, Jack Swilling, stored it away under his bed. When he awakened the next day, he learned to his sorrow that the Gila had overflowed its banks during the night and washed through his tent, carrying away his hard-earned gold.[4]

The peak year at Gila City probably was 1860. *Alta California*, a San Francisco newspaper, published a letter that year which suggests this was true. "Yesterday, I saw 152 ounces of gold from the Gila mines deposited with the agent of Wells-Fargo," wrote their correspondent from Fort Yuma. "Very beautiful it was; and there is more in the same country and 400 men digging for it . . . "[5]

Two other small mining camps sprang up not far from Gila City. Oroville was three miles east. Some coarse placer gold was found along the river at that point. Hardly anything is known about the camp except that it did exist at one time.

Las Flores was a small camp across the river and about three miles north of Gila City. This camp, on the fringes of the Laguna Mountains, seems to have been started by Mexicans and Indians who found Gila City inhospitable. They panned the area for a few years until someone found the source of the placer dust in a vein or two on the mountain side. A small crushing mill was erected there in 1870 to process the ore and newspaper accounts suggest that mining continued in the area for many years afterward. A few adobe walls were still visible

[4]Eldred O. Wilson, *Geology and Mineral Deposits of Southern Yuma County, Arizona* (Tucson: University of Arizona, 1933), p. 217.
[5]June 17, 1860.

Gila City placers were here.

—*Frank Love Photo.*

at Las Flores in the 1930s, but they have since vanished. Geological survey maps show numerous old shafts in the vicinity.

The boom at Gila City didn't last long. It was all over by 1862. When J. Ross Browne visited the site in 1864, he was able to find only "three chimneys and a coyote." A flood the year before had washed away all the buildings, and the miners had deserted for the more profitable gold fields in Central Arizona. Nearly a half million dollars in gold had been sifted from the gravel along the river.

Most histories of Gila City suggest that it ceased to exist by 1864. This is partly true since the original mining town had been washed away by that time. But Gila City was resurrected eventually, only to die again.

An outfit calling itself the "Gila City Gravel Mining Company" was first to announce it would try. Its promoters saw the possibilities of working the area using the more efficient hydraulic mining methods being pioneered in California during the late Seventies. A brief mention of their plans appeared in the *Mining and Scientific Press* in 1878, but they never seem to have gotten beyond the planning stage.[6]

A Missouri newspaper editor, George "Buck" Kelley, was the first person to seriously put the California methods to the test. Armed with capital from his Moberly, Missouri, publishing business, Kelley brought in expensive pumps to siphon water from the river and spray it onto the gravel banks under pressure. When all his new equipment was in place, he invited several Yuma dignitaries out to Gila City to see the beginning of the enterprise. The sheriff, M. J. Nugent; the county assessor, William Werninger; and the district attorney, Sam Purdy, all accepted the invitation even though the event took place at 7 a.m. on the morning of April 4, 1891.

Kelley's placer operation provided immediate employment for a number of laborers at Gila City, and the dormant town revived. A school was opened to educate the children of the area, with Miss Eula Bixby, a California school marm, presid-

[6]Mar. 2, 1878.

ing. Things looked so rosy that Kelley extended an invitation to the President of the United States, Benjamin Harrison, to drop by for a visit if he happened to pass that way. Local papers do not record that Harrison ever accepted his offer.

It was evident within a few months that Kelley's bonanza at Gila City was actually more in the nature of a white elephant. When Werninger, the county assessor, visited Gila City on his rounds a year later, he found the pumps shut down and the workers laid off. Some families were destitute. A few of the men had resorted to dry washing the gravel for gold, and were having some success. One of the men told him that he had taken out nearly $100 in gold in a few days. "The gold is there," Werninger told the *Sentinel*, "and the dry washers succeed in saving it, which it seemed the pumping-mining plant failed to do."[7]

Dry washing turned out to be only a temporary solution to the plight of Kelley's former employees. By October, Miss Bixby was passing out cast-off clothing that she had solicited from her friends in California to the poverty-stricken children.

With such a lack of employment, Gila City was bound to die a second time, but several ghastly murders probably hastened the exodus. The victims were A. S. Potter, postmaster of a recently established office there, and his unemployed friend, Robert Roberts. Passersby discovered Roberts propped up on a chair at the post office. He was dead, and an examination of the body suggested that he had been killed by a blow on the head from a rock or club. Horrified at their discovery, the finders left to inform the authorities and then found the body of Potter lying some twenty-five feet from the building. His head had also been crushed, and a bloody rock close by appeared to be the murder weapon.

The shocking discoveries had not ended with those revelations. Alarmed by the news that two men had been killed at Gila City, relatives of Frank Coz became concerned because they hadn't heard from him recently. They went to his ranch,

[7]*Arizona Sentinel,* Apr. 30, 1892.

across the river from Gila City, and found him lying dead several hundred yards from his house. An empty pistol lying nearby led officers to speculate that Coz had argued with Potter and Roberts, and had killed them. Filled with remorse, he may have shot himself. Not everyone accepted the official explanation. Some people blamed all three killings on Indians who recently had been driven away from Gila City.

The murders were never officially solved, and the crimes had the effect of frightening people away. Within a month, Hiram Monts, who had been employed by Kelley to guard his equipment, reported that "things are pretty quiet." He said that his nearest neighbor was two miles away, and that he hardly ever saw any other Anglos.

Kelley was determined not to let his bad investment turn into a complete loss. He returned to Gila City in December 1893, with a potential buyer in tow. His prospect was Judge Sanderson from his home town in Missouri. The judge denied that he was personally interested in the placers, and claimed to represent certain eastern interests. The deal failed to materialize, but later developments suggested that the interested party was really the judge.[8]

Kelley kept trying. Early the following year, he was in Denver trying to peddle his mine. The *Denver State Mining Record* took note of his visit to the Colorado capital and reported that he had visited with W. F. Hendricks, who happened to be a broker at the Denver Mining Exchange.[9] Within a few weeks, Gila City was visited by a number of prospective purchasers, including a Salt Lake City mine engineer and groups of capitalists from Denver and Los Angeles.

The Moberly editor knew the value of good publicity as well as anyone and he kept dropping hints from time to time that he was on the verge of reopening his mines and reaping a golden harvest. A typical example occurred during his trip to Yuma in December 1894, accompanied by another Missouri news-

[8]The *Arizona Sentinel*, 1891-1894, records the story of "Buck" Kelley's resurrection of Gila City.
[9]The Denver Journal was quoted in the *Arizona Sentinel*, Feb. 10, 1894.

was there to repair his Gila City equipment and that within a few weeks he would be "taking out gold by the shovels full."

It began to look as if his persistence had paid off in 1896. Sanderson suddenly returned to Yuma and announced that he had leased Kelley's claim.[10] A few months later, Sanderson returned to Missouri and gave up his dreams of wealth in Arizona. Kelley again was owner of the Gila City placers.

There were several other ill-fated efforts to mine the Gila City placers. Two Los Angeles men, L. H. Jones and E. C. Pointer, laid claim to 40 acres of placer ground near the Kelley claims in 1901. They informed the *Yuma Sun* that they had run a series of tests on the gravel which showed a yield of $2 a yard.[11] Nothing ever came of their venture, and the entire operation may have been a phony stock selling deal.

One promoter may have been in earnest. Peter W. Fleming, member of a Tucson law firm, joined forces with an investor cousin, Charles Fleming. The pair formed the Darius Green Mining Company, which established a claim at Gila City. The inventor cousin had developed a "gold extractor" which they hoped would separate the gold from the gravel along the river. They placered the area for several months, until Charles finally decided that his marvelous invention didn't really work.

The "Gold Placer Prospecting Association," formed in California in 1904, also announced plans to operate mines at Gila City. Its promoters claimed they were going to build a reservoir and pipe water from the river. They said the drop from the reservoir to the mines would give them adequate pressure to work the placer deposits. There is no indication that they ever carried through with their plans, and it seems likely that the entire scheme was designed to ensnare San Francisco and Los Angeles investors.

In 1904 Buck Kelley did manage to unload his mine. Three men, Ford, Anderson, and Ladd took it over, and announced

[10]*Arizonal Sentinel*, Mar. 31, 1896; Dec. 1 and 26, 1896.
[11]*The Yuma Sun*, May 3, 1901.

they had the solution to the water pressure problem. Rather than draw water from the river, they planned to dig a well at the mine site.[12] This scheme must have failed because there was no further mention of it in the newspapers.

[12]*Arizona Sentinel,* Apr. 6, 1904; Feb. 1, 1905.

Miners in the lower Colorado area, undated.

—*Courtesy Yuma County Historical Society.*

Chapter Three

BUSTLING LA PAZ — NOW ONLY A MEMORY

"La Paz . . . is a busy commercial town of adobe buildings with a population about equally American and Spanish," the *New York Tribune* told its readers in 1865. "It has some stores that would not do discredit to San Francisco . . ."[1]

The reference was to the busy Colorado River port a few miles north of the present village of Ehrenberg, Arizona. The *Tribune* was overstating the truth, but the mistake is understandable. Their information had come from an occasional correspondent with an ax to grind, Richard McCormick. He had just been appointed Secretary of State for the newly created Territory of Arizona and it was important to keep Easterners convinced that the frontier land was filling rapidly.

The truth about La Paz is more easily discovered in the yellowing *La Paz Miscellaneous Records* at the Yuma County (Arizona) Courthouse. They contain hundreds of deeds to La Paz town lots and nearby mining claims. Most of the owners had Mexican surnames rather than American. Morales, Bustamente, and Ortiz are common in those documents. The first dozen or so pages disclose only three non-Mexican names.

McCormick was right about there being stores in La Paz, but they hardly rivaled the commercial enterprises of San Francisco. A San Francisco paper informed its readers in 1862 that a miner named Kelsey had given up placering to build stores and described the kind he was constructing. "The latter work is very simple; the counter, the chief article in the store being made of a few posts stuck in the ground, with a couple of straight boughs laid across, and then covered with pieces of a

[1]*New York Tribune,* June 1, 1865.

packing box," reported the poper. "Nails are not used at all. The buildings are merely brush-covered frames . . ."[2]

La Paz owed its existence to the discovery of gold placers a few miles east of the river. The discoverer was Paulino Weaver, an old trail guide, who had been knocking around the Southwest for thirty years. Weaver had been attracted to Gila City by the gold discoveries there, but decided to go trapping up the Colorado when the diggings became unprofitable.

Weaver's trapping party was not long in finding that the valuable Sonoran beaver were in short supply and he began leaving the party to prospect. One day in January 1862 he wandered up El Arroyo de la Tinaja at the foot of La Paz Mountain and found a few small nuggets. As nuggets go, they didn't amount to much, and Weaver carried them back to camp without mentioning his find to the other trappers. He deposited them in a goose quill and dismissed the matter from his mind for the time.

When the trappers returned south, the party lingered for a time at Las Lagunas, where Laguna Dam is now located. José Maria Redondo, who operated a ferry that was used by Gila City miners who wished to cross the river, asked Weaver about his success in trapping upriver. The old trail guide replied that the beaver were scarce but showed the gold he had found.

The chispas that meant little to Weaver had a different effect on Redondo. Gold fever ran in his blood. Within hours after talking to Weaver, Redondo had provisioned an expedition and set out for the La Paz area.

His trip met with instant success. Two ounces of gold turned up in his pan less than a mile from the place Weaver had picked up his nuggets.

The news spread like wildfire. Mexicans who had been working at Gila City were first to reach the scene. Many were as lucky as Redondo had been. Don Juan Ferra quickly found a fifty-five ounce chispa that brought him more than $800. Others

[2]*Alta California*, July 30, 1862.

found smaller ones weighing as much as twenty-seven ounces. With gold selling for $18.50 an ounce in San Francisco, it looked as if there were fortunes to be made.

At least one person did make his fortune at La Paz. Manuel Ravenna, an Italian immigrant, began operating a store at La Paz. Part of his business involved buying gold from the La Paz miners at $16 an ounce and transporting it to San Francisco, along with the gold dust that had been exchanged for goods in his store. He realized a profit of $2 an ounce or more for this service.

While engaged in the mercantile trade, he had the opportunity to purchase a likely lode claim, the Conquest, about five miles from La Paz. He bought it and operated the mine several years and then sold it to an English firm. One source states that Ravenna got $2 million for it. But he hardly lived to enjoy his wealth because he died within a year of the sale.[3] There is no evidence that the English company was ever able to recover any of its investment in the Conquest.

Transportation was a serious problem. The old Butterfield Stage Line passed near La Paz before the Civil War, but removal of Union troops from Arizona at the start of the war spelled the death warrant of the company. Some of the first miners to reach La Paz followed the old stage route from San Diego, which went from San Diego to Vallecito, Warner's Ranch, Temecula, and Fort Yuma to the diggings.

Others sought shortcuts but sometimes found death in the desert instead. An Indian hired to carry letters from La Paz-bound miners to their folks in San Francisco reported that a family by the name of Garrett, numbering seven persons, had perished along the way. Another party of five, led by Charles Yates, died in the desert. A group headed by Wallace Woodworth nearly met the same fate even though they were following a route recommended by other parties. The trail did not lead to La Paz.

[3]*Ralph Mahoney*, "Our Italian-American Heritage," *Arizona Days and Ways*, Aug. 11, 1957, p. 10.

California newspapers reported the deaths on the trail faithfully but continued to fan the flames of gold fever by telling readers about the fortunes being made in the mining camp. *Alta California* informed its patrons that a man named Bennett had just returned from the mines and had immediately deposited one hundred ounces of gold in the Wells-Fargo safe. The San Francisco newspaper described one route which they affirmed was a safe one. It involved sailing for San Diego on the steamer *Senator*. Once in that city, they advised their readers to purchase a horse or mule, which would range in price from $25-$100, and follow the trail to Fort Yuma. Wells were located each ten or twenty miles along the way, and Fort Yuma was 140 miles from San Diego by that route.[4] From the military post, it was only another 90 miles to La Paz on a trail that paralleled the Colorado.

If *Alta's* information about the conveniently located wells was as much in error as their mileage statistics, many a traveler must have been sadder but wiser by the time he reached Fort Yuma. The present day interstate highway route covers a distance of 170 miles between Yuma and San Diego. It seems highly unlikely that a rough wagon road could have shortened the distance by 30 miles.

New routes were soon discovered. The most popular one was a trail blazed by William Bradshaw, a pioneer who has been described as "a natural lunatic." The Bradshaw route wasn't entirely new. It had previously been charted part way by a railroad survey party working in California, but Bradshaw was the first man to demonstrate that wagons could be hauled over it

Bradshaw found a shortcut that made the route feasible. Chief Cabazon, the head man of a desert Indian tribe, described a pass through the mountains at San Gorgonio to him. He found it and followed the bed of the Whitewater River down into the low desert where the Salton Sea is now located. At Dos Palmas, an oasis in the desert, he found water and relief from

[4]*Alta California*, July 2, 1862; July 27, 1862.

the sun. Leaving the oasis behind, he blazed a trail that roughly parallels today's Interstate 10 Highway. It brought him to the Colorado River about six miles south of La Paz.

Bradshaw took possession of the crossing and built a ferry to transport the swarms of miners he expected to follow his route. It was a wise move, and it made him wealthy in a few short years.[5] When quartz ledges were discovered on the Arizona side of the river in the fall of 1862, his ferry shack became the first building in Olive City, center of the Weaver Mining District. Like many other successful businessmen, Bradshaw had the urge to try his hand at politics, and declared himself a candidate for a seat in the First Territorial Legislature of Arizona. Charles Poston, a more experienced campaigner, beat him out, but it was not all a complete loss for the ferry operator. His friends in the law-making body granted him an exclusive ferry franchise.

Sudden wealth turned out to be too much for Bradshaw, and much of his fortune soon found its way into the hands of saloon keepers. Alcoholism brought him to a tragic end. He slit his throat in the winter of 1864 while suffering from a fit of delirium tremens. Olive City died shortly afterward, too. The mineral veins proved to be low grade ore. Nothing remains of the town, and few persons are even aware that it existed.

The diggings east of La Paz were mostly in gulches. One of the most important placer locations was about a mile north of the pass now used by Interstate Highway 10 where it passes through the Dome Rock Mountains between Quartzsite and Ehrenberg. It was known as "Ferra Gulch" in those days because Don Juan Ferra had discovered his fifty-five ounce chispa there. Another important site was northwest of Ferra Gulch, along the washes of Middle Camp Mountain. Closer to La Paz were the placers on Goodman Wash at the foot of La Paz Mountain.

Most miners used the old Mexican dry washing method to extract the gold. Water was too expensive. At Ferra's Gulch,

[5]J. Wilson McKenney, "Gold Builds a Road," *Desert Magazine*, Vol. 1, No. 2, December 1937, pp. 8-9.

water hauled from the river sold for 37½ cents a gallon. It was even more expensive at Middle Camp, since it had to be transported all the way from Tyson's Well (now Quartzsite). With men drinking from three to five gallons a day during the hot summer months, and the average laborer earning about eight dollars a day, there was no way the claim owners could profit from washing the gravel.

Dry washing was inefficient, but it wasn't very difficult. Gravel was scooped onto a sheet or blanket and tossed into the air, caught, and tossed into the air again. When a good breeze was blowing, the light material was quickly blown away, and the heavier material left. If the claim was a productive one, particles of gold remained when the process had been completed.

The town that developed west of the placers was named La Paz, Spanish for "the peace," because Weaver found gold on January 12, a day that Sonoran Catholics celebrated as the feast day of Our Lady of Peace. But peaceful it was not! Some of the worst American and Mexican desperadoes of the Southwest infested the town. A San Francisco newspaper reported that only one person in twelve or fifteen actually worked for a living. The rest sponged off those who did.[6]

One outlaw who terrorized the town was Boss Danewood, whose career in crime ended abruptly at the end of a hangman's rope in Los Angeles a few years later. Another killer who headquartered in La Paz was "Red" Kelly, a sharpshooting roughneck. Red gave riverboat captain Isaac Polhamus the scare of his life one day. The captain had been collecting freight to put aboard his steamer and was about to enter a store accompanied by a local gunfighter named "Texas." Someone suddenly called out, "Stand aside if you please, Captain. I'm going to kill that damned scoundrel!"

Polhamus ducked for cover just in time to avoid a hail of bullets from the gun of Red Kelly, who was crouching across the street. The unfortunate Texas did manage to draw his gun

[6]*Alta California*, Oct. 31, 1862.

and get off one or two shots at his assailant, but he soon fell dead in the street. The killer lit out for parts unknown, and was never punished for the murder.[7]

The Civil War was raging during the heydey of the La Paz placers. Though the town was located within the Union, it was a hotbed of Confederate sentiment. *Alta California* warned its readers, in January 1863, that Bob Groom and Don Showalter had formed a Rebel guerrilla band of nearly a hundred members at La Paz. The organization was said to be training in Sonora and planning a raid on Federal troops at Tucson.[8] The raid never materialized and may have been a figment of the imagination of some reporter. Bob Groom's exposure as a Confederate sympathizer doesn't seem to have done him any harm. He was elected to the Territorial Legislature shortly afterward.

At least two killings in La Paz can be traced to the Confederate leanings of some of its residents. Two Union soldiers, Privates Wentworth and Behn of the 4th California Infantry, were murdered by a Secessionist named Edwards while walking on the street in La Paz on May 22, 1863. Troops enroute from Fort Mohave to Fort Yuma recovered the bodies the next day.[9] The shootings led the army to station a detachment of troops at La Paz, and there were no more incidents. Edwards took to the desert after the killings. He escaped the legal penalty for his crime, but paid a heavier one. In his haste to clear out of La Paz, he didn't take enough water, and died in the desert from thirst.[10]

[7]H. P. Wood, "The Gold Fields of La Paz," *The Silver Gate*, Feb. 1900. Information taken from typescript of original in files of Yuma Historical Society; page numbers not recorded on typescript.

[8]*Alta California*, Jan. 28, 1863.

[9]*Fort Yuma Post Returns*, May 1863.

[10]*Alta California*, Aug. 2, 1863. There is another version of this incident. It relates that Edwards continued living at La Paz after the murders and went unpunished for his crime. After the Civil War, a buddy of the murdered soldiers appeared one day at La Paz, sought Edwards out, and gunned him down while he was at work in the diggings. In light of the *Alta* report and the fact that Union troops were stationed in the town after the incident, the second version seems to be a figment of romantic nonsense.

With desperadoes the likes of Kelly, Danewood, and Edwards about, the residents of La Paz soon began to recognize a need for law and order. A provisional government was organized as early as December 1862, and permanent officials were chosen less than a year later.

A character known as "Six-toed" Pete Badilla was elected sheriff during the latter elections. He seems an unlikely choice when one takes into account an article regarding his activities that had appeared in the newspapers a year earlier. According to *Alta California*, the future law officer appeared at a camp of miners who were bound for La Paz one summer day in 1862. Here is a description of the incident:

But on this grateful morning of Monday, June 23rd, an individual known among the sporting fraternity of Los Angeles as "Six-toed" Pete arrived at our camp, fresh from the Colorado River. Not being intimately acquainted with Pete, I cannot of my own knowledge and belief swear that the said Pete is the actual possessor of that extra member on his foot; whether it is his right foot or left foot; or on both feet; but this I am willing to affirm, that Six-toed Pete has studied human nature sufficiently well to know that welcome news makes a welcome guest. So Pete told big stories backed by big lumps of bright yellow gold, and so Pete became the lion of the hour—for he had been there; had taken out gold, and had gold to amount to several hundred dollars (a part of which I saw and "hefted") with him to show for it . . .

But Pete's laurels were shortlived and soon withered and dried up under the influence of the accounts brought by José Antonio Sanchez . . . and a number of others who arrived at our camp during the day . . . When he heard what Six-toed Pete had told us, he waxed wroth, and went down to the next camp where that individual was basking in the sunshine of his popularity under the shade of a tree, and told him as they say in Spanish "claidades" but as Sanchez translated it in English, "I give him Jessie." For according to Sanchez's statement, Pete never went to the diggings, but had lain about the pueblo on the river, doing nothing but laying traps to get some Sonoreno storekeepers to play a little game of monte with him. He finally succeeded in corralling them and got their cash, coin, and gold dust, and then he "dusted" for Los Angeles.[11]

[11]*Alta California*, July 30, 1862.

The pueblo on the river grew rapidly as miners poured into the area. It soon was able to boast a billiard parlor, numerous bars, several stores, and even a bull ring. Regular stage service to Los Angeles was available on a weekly basis by October 1862. A fare of $40 was charged for the trip. Supplies were generally brought from California to the mouth of the Colorado by the steamer *Senator* and then carried upriver by one of the boats belonging to Captain George Johnson's Colorado River Steamboat Company.

An 1863 visitor to La Paz, calling himself "A Frontiersman," has left an account of life there. He described crossing the desert by mule from San Bernardino to arrive in La Paz at breakfast time. After leaving his mule at a corral, he visited a bakery operated by a German, where he was able to purchase a breakfast of bread, coffee, and tough steak as well as water for a bath.

Fortified with a mining camp breakfast, the traveler sallied out to do the town. He observed numerous men lounging in the doorways of saloons, or simply squatting in the street. A number of Mohave Indian men were about wearing breech clouts while the females of the tribe were dressed in skirts that reached their knees. The Indians seemed amused to observe the ill-humor of newly arrived Americans frantically hustling about trying to find a place to sleep or attempting to procure water and hay for their animals.

Later in his visit, the "Frontiersman" attended a show held by two traveling Mexican tight rope walkers and a clown. They charged their customers $1 apiece to view the show in their tent. He also witnessed a bull fight at the arena, but commented that attendance was poor. The fact that no matador had ever been known to lose his life in the La Paz ring seemed an explanation for the sparse crowd. Foot races among the local Indians were another means of enjoyment that he noted. Races were held in the city streets, and wagering was quite heavy. To the visitor's surprise, some of the heaviest bettors were Indians.[12]

[12]Bancroft's *Arizona Scraps*, Vol. 2, pp. 500-501.

La Paz eventually had its own newspaper, the *La Paz Gazette*. It was published in 1866 and possibly in 1867. There are no known copies still in existence, so information is lacking on this journalistic endeavor. The only evidence still extant regarding this forgotten paper is excerpts copied from it in other publications.

The town was the county seat of Yuma County until 1871. It had a courthouse, an assay office directed by Herman Ehrenberg, and money was appropriated by the Territorial Legislature to operate a school, providing local citizens would match the territorial funds. La Paz seems to have neglected this opportunity to educate its children.

In truth, La Paz began to decline as early as 1863 when it was just getting started well. Pauline Weaver found gold in Central Arizona that summer. The news led to an immediate exodus from western Arizona to central Arizona. That didn't mean the extinction of the town because it continued to be a river port where goods were unloaded for shipment overland to the new diggings.

The meandering and often treacherous Colorado finally killed La Paz. It left its old bed and cut itself a new course in 1870, leaving the river port high and dry a mile or so from the new channel. La Paz became as obsolete as the dinosaur, and Ehrenberg a few miles south, which had sixteen residents in 1863, took its place as a shipping point for cargoes going east.

The old adobe buildings gradually wore down and melted away. When George Nock visited the site in 1887, he recorded that the old courthouse and a few other buildings were still partially standing.[13] These remnants are now gone. The author visited La Paz in Spring 1971, and could hardly find any evidence it had ever existed.

There is hope that La Paz may live again. The Colorado River Indian Tribes have recently announced their plan to excavate the ruins, which are on their reservation. Perhaps they will restore the old mining town. Let's hope they do. Old La Paz should not simply be forgotten.

[13]"Recollections of George W. Nock," ed. by Henry Pickering Walker, *Arizona and the West*, Vol. IX, No. 2, p. 167.

CHAPTER FOUR

IF LEAD WERE ONLY GOLD

But in the wildest soaring
In romantic fiction's field,
Mind had never figured
What mine eyes did behold.
'Neath that castelated dome
Where earth herself had seated
The home of her great king,
The royal King of Gold![1]
—Author Unknown.

THE sentimental tripe printed above was the final verse of a long maudlin poem that was published in a Yuma newspaper in 1881. Its author evidently meant to glamorize Castle Dome Peak, the unusual landmark that soars skyward northeast of Yuma. The unknown poet seemed to be laboring under the impression that the scores of mines which dotted the foothills around the mountain were gold mines. John Dorrington, editor of the paper which printed the ode, certainly knew better, since he dabbled in mining. If the Castle Dome mines had produced gold rather than lead and small quantities of silver, Yuma County would have been the mining wonder of the world. Between 1870 and 1949, nearly eighteen million pounds of lead came out of them.

No one knows the identity of the persons who first mined at Castle Dome. The only certainty is that it was not the Americans who formed a mining district there during the early part of the Civil War. Newspapers from that era state that prospectors looked for "old works" or cuts which showed signs of an

[1]*Arizona Sentinel,* Oct. 22, 1891.

earlier mining operation. Among the mines which were actually older diggings were the Bright Star, Mammoth, Silver Age, Castle Dome, and Splendid Ophir.

There is also some mystery regarding the identity of the American who first discovered ore in the district. Yuma's pioneer newspaper, the *Sentinel*, said in 1881 that they were located by William P. Blake. It said he found them in 1863 but had been driven away by Indians. Later in 1869, according to the *Sentinel* article, someone remembered Blake's discovery and filed claims on it.[2]

The *Sentinel* was badly misinformed. Blake was not even in Arizona in 1863. He was in Oakland, where he was Professor of Minerology, Geology, and Mining at the new College of California.[3] Even if he had been in Arizona in 1863, it would have been too late to discover the Castle Dome mines because they had already been located. Documents in the County Recorder's Office at Yuma show quite clearly that claims were filed at Castle Dome in 1862. Blake's name does not appear anywhere in those records. To cinch the argument, one needs to only point out that Blake personally thought Jacob Snively had been one of the original discoverers, and said so in print.[4]

There is much evidence to support the contention that Jacob Snively was the discoverer. Snively was named chairman of the miners' meeting which established the district. It seems likely that such an honor would be awarded to the locator of the first mine. His name is included among the owners of the first several claims recorded. Add to this the fact that one of the prominent mountains in the Castle Dome Range is labeled "Mt. Snively" on an 1864 map of the district, and it seems fairly certain that it was the Texan who first found silver beneath the Dome.

There was no concern at all with mining lead at Castle Dome in 1862. Silver was the attraction, and no one seemed to care

[2]*Arizona Sentinel*, Dec. 24, 1881.
[3]*Daily Evening Bulletin* (San Francisco), Jan. 23, 1864.
[4]Blake, W. P., *Castle Dome Mining and Smelting Company* (private report), New Haven, Conn., July 1880.

that the argentiferous galena they were digging from the earth contained as much as 70% lead. Even if they had cared, there was no way to get it to one of the West Coast smelters or to Wales in Great Britain to reduce the ore profitably.

News soon leaked out about Snively's find at Castle Dome, and prospectors began descending on the area to stake out claims. It took an entire book to list the claims filed during the first year. No one seemed to know that most of them were worthless, considering the state of mining technology in 1863.

A correspondent from the *Alta California* with the pen name of "Voyageur" was unimpressed by what he found in the district in 1863. He reported to his readers that a mine called the "Wide World" wasn't really wide at all. He found it to contain a vein of ore only 10 inches across. Only the "Ophir" made much of an impression. It had a ledge of galena about 5 feet wide and he thought it might be worth mining.

Two towns began to sprout as a result of the silver strike. Castle Dome Landing was established by Snively, A. Bowman, and R. F. Mastin, in June 1863. The trio laid claim to 640 acres at the river for a steamboat landing which would serve as a shipping point for Castle Dome ore. Four or five houses were built at the landing within a year, and a wagon road was built from there to the mines.

Castle Dome City was established at the foot of Mt. Ophir, in the approximate center of the area now dotted with abandoned mine shafts. It wasn't much as cities go and "Voyageur" found a population of only ten men and two women inhabiting the two tents and one brush house in the metropolitan area. The thing that seems to have impressed him most was the rabidly Secessionist attitude of the inhabitants. He warned his readers that "sleek and oily Black Republicans" had better stay out of Castle Dome City, and advised such persons to take "the back trail to the fort." Fort Yuma was garrisoned by Union troops, and it may be guessed that they were not much appreciated by the residents of the mining camp.

Jacob Snively was serving as recorder for the district at that time, but the city reporter was shocked by the appearance of

Deserted mining company headquarters at Castle Dome.

—*Frank Love Photo.*

his "office." It was out in the open, in an arroyo, with no shelter. His belongings were all piled on the ground, and a signpost informed the public that "This is the Recorder's Office!" His gear consisted of a battered valise, a box labeled "Olive Oil," which functioned as a desk, a pot, frying pan, shotgun, and several blankets.[5]

Hope was high that Castle Dome City would become a large mining camp, and this ambition soon received a boost. A charter was granted for construction of a railroad to the mines. San Francisco investors began appearing on the scene after reports were circulated that the Mammoth Lode contained ore that assayed $103 a ton silver, $70 léad, and $12 in gold.[6] By April 1864, almost a hundred mines were being developed or worked.

The San Francisco promoters were impressed by what they saw, and hastened to cash in on the boom. In one two month period in 1864, no less than five speculative combines filed certificates of incorporation indicating an intent to operate Castle Dome mines. The Castle Dome Mining Company was first to file, and reported capital stock of $180,000. Less than two weeks later, the Arizona Consolidated Mining Company entered the lists, to be followed shortly afterward by the Fortuna Silver Mining Company, Henry Clay Mining Company, and Buena Plata Consolidation Mining Company.[7] Then the boom suddenly collapsed!

Castle Dome died in 1865 in spite of the fact that there was rich galena in the mountains. What caused its failure?

Several possibilities suggest themselves. The San Francisco speculators may not have been as interested in producing ore as in selling stock. Lack of good transportation to the mines made them a highly expensive venture for anyone truly interested in large scale mining. A railroad would have helped, but it never got out of the planning stages. Steamship transpor-

[5]*Alta California*, Jan. 2, 1864.

[6]*Alta California*, Feb. 23, 1864; *Daily Evening Bulletin* (San Francisco), Jan. 21, 1864.

[7]*Daily Evening Bulletin* (San Francisco), Jan. 21; Feb. 2, 3, 11; Mar. 19, 1864.

tation was still undependable in 1865, and freight rates were prohibitive.

Another factor working against Castle Dome was the richer gold strike in Central Arizona that drew miners away. The Walker Diggings, the Vulture, Big Bug, and Lynx Creek mines offered a far better chance of striking it rich than one might find digging argentiferous galena. As the news from the Prescott area got better and better, it was difficult to find anyone who wanted to mine the silver-lead ore in Western Arizona.

But the district was only in a state of hibernation, that ended when the rising demand for lead reawakened it. In the spring of 1869, Jack Hamilton of Arizona City (Yuma) and two brothers named Butterfield, recalled that the ore at Castle Dome not only contained silver, but also high percentages of lead. They reopened one of the old veins and were soon finding enough high grade galena to ship it all the way to a smelter in San Francisco and still show a profit.

Word was soon out that the Hamilton-Butterfield ore contained $40-$60 a ton in silver, and was also producing lead at a rate of 1,000 pounds per ton. Others hastened to restake the old claims, and some new mines were found. But the most exciting by far was an older claim, the Flora Temple. It dated back to 1863, and *Mining and Scientific Press* reported that its operator, Nick Gunther, was likely to get $90 a ton for the 400 tons he had ready for shipment in August 1871.[8] In the next few years, another 20,000 tons of galena came from the same mine.

The success of men like Hamilton, Gunter, and the Butterfields led the miners to reorganize the district. William P. Miller, a Pennsylvania lawyer, was the guiding spirit when the operators met in one of their cabins at 8 p.m. on July 17, 1871. The twelve men attending the meeting declared all prior mining laws void, and agreed to grant a claim to anyone who

[8]*Mining and Scientific Press*, May 8, 1869; Aug. 5, 1871.

sank a 15 foot shaft. In recognition of Miller's efforts, he was appointed district recorder.[10]

Mining was on a stable and profitable basis within a few years. Forty men were at work for three different companies by 1874, and the *Sentinel* editorialized that the mines would "never peter out" again. The paper attributed the earlier collapse of the district to the haphazard and superficial methods earlier miners had used, and suggested that the present operators were men of "intelligence" and "energy."[11]

Older methods of handling ore did not disappear rapidly in spite of the *Sentinel's* optimism. Ore was still being crushed by the ancient arrastra, a device which utilized heavy stones to pulverize the metal-bearing rock. The product of the arrastra was smelted in adobe furnaces and emerged as a "plancha," a bar of metal composed of about 95% lead, ½% silver, and a small amount of impurities. Mexican entrepreneurs operated most of the smelters, and charged the miners $40 a ton for their services.

A first step toward modernization came in 1875 when George Nagle erected a more efficient smelter, which could reduce forty tons of ore per day. California capitalists got into the picture a few years later at the behest of William Miller. By 1877 they could no longer ignore the steady flow of planchas from the Castle Dome Smelter, and formed the Castle Dome Smelting and Mining Company at San Francisco.

Miller had convinced the Californians that the recently completed railroad to Yuma, the Southern Pacific, offered new opportunities to profit from the galena mines. It was no longer economical to smelt the ore in the district, he told them. Rather than import charcoal to run the Arizona smelter, and transport the planchas to the coast, it would be more economical to ship high grade ore to a California smelter. The smelters at San Francisco were willing to pay $55 a ton for ore that assayed between $60-$75. Costs would be as follows:

[11]*Arizona Sentinel*, Jan. 17, 1874; Jan. 31, 1874.
[10]*Book of Mines, Castle Dome:* 1871-1875, Office of the County Recorder, Yuma County (Arizona) Courthouse.

Mining	$ 9.00 per ton
Sacks and sacking...............	2.00
Hauling ore to river.............	7.00
Transportation to San Francisco...	11.00
	————
Total costs......	$29.00 per ton

A profit of $26.00 a ton was possible.[12] Miller said he was willing to sell his claims to the combine and become mining superintendent. The investors accepted his offer, and began buying up claims.

Some old prospectors saw the situation as a golden opportunity to get rid of mines where the ore was nearly exhausted. Lige Bettis, a veteran miner who owned both the Pocahontas and Arkansaw Mines, knew a good thing when he saw one. Neither of his mines had been timbered, and he had taken thousands of tons of ore from them. The Arkansaw was already down 275 feet.

The new firm had scarcely taken over Bettis's claims before they discovered that they would have to timber them. Several shafts had caved in because of heavy rains. To make matters more serious, they had only gone 25 feet farther into the Arkansaw when they struck water. Fearful that they had tapped an underground river, mining expert William Blake was called to the scene to render his professional opinion. After visiting the Arkansaw in April 1879, he was able to assure them that the water was really seepage from recent rains. Blake had planned to render a chemical analysis of the water, but that was made impossible when a thirsty burro drank the sample he had procured while he was eating breakfast.

The Pocahontas also caused problems for the new owners. A fire broke out at the 175 foot level in January 1881, and two miners nearly perished from smoke inhalation. One of them had carelessly left a candle burning on a timber, and it set the shaft afire.

[12]*Bancroft's Arizona Scraps*, Vol. 2, pp. 407-408. Clipping labeled "*Bulletin*," Dec. 11, 1878."

A few independent miners refused to sell out to the San Francisco firm, and tried to continue operations as before. They found themselves harassed by the company to such an extent that the editor of the *Sentinel* felt compelled to editorialize on the corporation's activities. He wrote that the Castle Dome Smelting and Mining Company had "given the world to know that they control the whole district and no room is left for the coming prospector." He complained that William Miller, the company superintendent, was acting as if "he owns the entire country."[13]

Castle Dome had its share of fights and shootings, but it probably was never as bad as Hedges or Fortuna. One of its most exciting manhunts began on May 28, 1881, when Rafael Gutierrez was shot to death by a desperado calling himself "Blanco Flores." The killer fled Castle Dome right after the shooting. Witnesses told law officers that he was about twenty-three years old, "boyish and quite handsome." Investigation of the crime disclosed that the gunman was a fugitive who was using an alias for his real name, which was Florencia Sanchez. The mining company offered a $50 reward for his capture.

Sanchez had fled toward Yuma, and decided that he was safe once he passed through town and crossed the river into California. He found employment working for Hall Hanlon, a rancher who operated a ferry for persons wishing to cross the Colorado. Someone informed Yuma County Sheriff Tyner of Sanchez' whereabouts, and the law officer set out with his deputy, Walter Millar, to take him into custody. When the officers arrived at the ferry landing, they spied Sanchez out in the river on the ferry. He saw them at about the same time, dived into the river, and swam downstream, where he was able to escape in some underbrush. Tyner returned to town and got some Indian trackers, while his deputy continued the search. The trackers lost no time in finding the fugitive's trail and soon caught up with him. When Sanchez jumped into the river a

[13]*Arizona Sentinel*, Sept. 21, 1878; May 3, 1879; Jan. 29, 1881; July 9, 1881.

Flora Temple Mine and Mill at Castle Dome. (N.D.)

—Courtesy Yuma County Historical Society.

second time to escape capture, Millar opened fire and shot him dead.[14]

Marijuana played a role in one Castle Dome shooting affray. Barbaro Hernandez, a miner, who others claimed had been smoking the weed, opened fire on several miners as they were descending a shaft on January 20, 1898. His bullets missed, but he told bystanders that he would return later and shoot more accurately. His intended victims had stolen a windlass belonging to him, he said.

The aggrieved men let the matter pass for that day, but paid an early morning visit to the Hernandez cabin several days later. They said they only wanted to talk the matter over, but took along a gun to encourage conversation. Hernandez did his share of the talking with a shotgun he had loaded for the occasion, and wounded both of his visitors. Much to the dismay of the injured men, a grand jury refused to indict Hernandez, who claimed he acted in self defense.[15]

Prostitution was another source of trouble at Castle Dome. Too much booze and infatuation with a camp whore proved fatal to one Juan Trego on New Year's Day, 1901. When the unfortunate man had an argument with a prostitute he fancied, another admirer invited him outside for a talk. As Trego stepped outside the door, the second man shot him dead. No one admitted knowing the name of the killer, who immediately fled and was never apprehended. The *Sentinel* did not seem especially perturbed about Trego's passing, and remarked that he had a bad reputation in Yuma and had recently completed a jail sentence for selling liquor to Indians.[16]

With so many men carrying guns, and willing to use them, mine superintendents often found their job an exciting one. Ed Mayes, one of the Castle Dome superintendents, found himself looking into the barrel of a six-shooter when he tried to fire Trinidad Reyes for being drunk on the job in March 1899.

[14]*Arizona Sentinel*, June 4, 1881; July 30, 1881.
[15]*Yuma Sun*, Jan. 28, 1898; Apr. 22, 1898.
[16]*Ibid.*, Jan. 4, 1901. Trego was mistakenly identified as Juan Llego, while the *Arizona Sentinel* identified him as Juan Trego on January 9.

Abandoned Castle Dome mine.

—*Frank Love Photo.*

Reyes managed to get one shot off at Mayes, but the superintendent was able to deflect his aim with his hand and disarm him. Reyes immediately fled to Mexico.

Abram Molina, a Yuma County deputy sheriff, heard that Reyes was just across the border from Pima County several months later, and made plans to capture him. He was somehow able to trick the fugitive into returning to the United States, and arrested him.[17] But it was to no avail. Reyes managed to slip the iron bolts out of several adobe blocks in the county jail, and fled back to Mexico during a sandstorm.

The Castle Dome Mining and Smelting Company was dependent on high grade ore for a profitable operation. By 1884 most of the best galena had been extracted, and the company closed down. Independent miners began relocating claims they had allowed to lapse, and mining resumed. Frank Vomocil and Paul Billicke, two experienced silver miners, were first to realize the possible profits in shipping low grade galena. With no investors demanding dividends, an experienced miner might keep a crew working regularly and get a good return for his efforts. The two men relocated eight of the old claims, and had a crew of seventeen working regularly by 1891.[18]

Gandolfo and Sanguinetti, a pair of Yuma merchants, also took up claims and set a crew to work. One of the mines they reopened was the old Pocahontas, which they rechristened the "Lola." Nearly fifty men were employed by the various mines they operated. Local butchers saw the opportunity too. The Hodges Brothers, owners of a Yuma meat market, took over the Esperanza and American Mines.[19]

Mining operations continued at a high level of production throughout the Nineties. The continuing success of local businessmen attracted a group of Chicago capitalists in 1897. The combine formed the Castle Dome Mining Company, and bonded thirteen claims owned by Gandolfo and Sanguinetti, and seven owned by Vomocil. When a trial run of several months failed to

[17]*Arizona Sentinel*, Mar. 25, 1899; May 27, 1899.
[18]*Ibid.*, July 22, 1891.
[19]*Ibid.*, July 20, 1895.

Castle Dome, 1972.

—*Frank Love Photo.*

show a profit, the capitalists allowed their options to lapse, and withdrew.[20]

Shortly afterward, William and Eliza Luce began buying up Castle Dome claims with the fortune they had garnered across the river in the Cargo Muchacho District. The Luce's had earned their wealth using a new gold extraction method, the cyanide process, which had come to America from Scotland in the early Nineties.

Before the discovery of the new method, gold and silver ore was treated in stamp mills, where it was pulverized to facilitate removal of the metal. While the stamp mills did the job to a degree, the tailings left over from the process still contained much gold or silver. There being no effective way to remove the metal, the refuse was discarded near stamp mills and often formed small mountains. With discovery of the cyanide process, those privy to its secrets began buying up mine tailings and reaping a golden harvest.

Luce was first to understand the possible profits lying in the old tailings dumps around the Lower Colorado. His first move was to buy the dump at the old El Rio Mill, which had processed gold ore from the Cargo Muchacho Mines for a decade or so. There were nearly 800,000 tons of tailings lying at the mill site near the bend of the river, and much of it still contained gold worth $5.00 a ton. He worked the entire dump at a cost of $1.50 a ton, managing to extract a high percentage of the gold.

Having acquired many of the claims at Castle Dome, the Luce's formed the Castle Dome Mining and Milling Company in May 1899. It is quite likely that they were more interested in the tailings around the district than the nearly exhausted mines. The cyanide process worked nearly as well on silver tailings as on gold, and they soon constructed a 200 ton plant and began working the refuse piles.

The Luce's operation wasn't without its quota of problems. They accused their Mexican employees of making off with some of the better ore, and asked the local constable, Pete Burke, to

[20]*Yuma Sun*, July 30, 1897.

Old mining machinery at Castle Dome.

—*Frank Love Photo.*

investigate in January 1901. The law officer traveled to the mines, accompanied by his deputy, Billy Horan, but was unable to catch anyone stealing and had to return to Yuma with no one under arrest.

The hot Arizona climate never had much appeal for William Luce, head of the clan, and the Alaska gold rush offered him an opportunity to escape its rigors. He turned the Castle Dome operation over to his wife and son Robert, a graduate of the California School of Mines, and headed for the Yukon.[21]

Departure of the elder Luce marked the end of an era. With the tailings dumps depleted and only very low quality galena coming from the mines, it was difficult for the mother and son team to keep solvent. The *Sentinel* records that they were soon in financial difficulties, with the Sanguinetti firm attaching their property for non-payment of bills in September 1902. Compounding their difficulties were divorce proceedings that Mrs. Luce filed against her absent husband the next spring. A decree was granted in April 1903.[22]

Mining operations ceased at Castle Dome in 1906, and the mines were idle until the demand for lead revived them during World War I. But when the war ended, they closed again and remained shut down for more than twenty years. World War II brought the price of lead up, and they reopened under the direction of George and Kenneth Holmes. The brothers produced three million pounds of lead in 1943.

Mrs. Luce was still living at Castle Dome when a writer from *The Desert Magazine* visited the mines during the war. He wrote of her as "the guardian goddess" of Castle Dome, and commented that her faith in the mines remained constant when they were closed for so many years. The magazine published her picture, with the famous Dome landmark as a backdrop.[23]

[21]*Arizona Sentinel*, July 4, 1896; Aug. 25, 1899; Nov. 25, 1899; Feb. 6, 1901; Aug. 28, 1901.

[22]*Ibid.*, Apr. 8, 1903; Sept. 24, 1902.

[23]John W. Hilton, "Nuggets to Bullets at Castle Dome," *The Desert Magazine*, VII, 12 (October 1944), pp. 5-9.

The mines closed temporarily when the war ended, but they came to life again. A small firm was mining galena and florite when the author visited there in February 1972. A miner reported that florite was bringing $90 a ton, and that one car load of galena sold for $140 a ton the summer before. An El Paso smelter was handling the ore.

Wouldn't it be great if all that lead were gold?

CHAPTER FIVE

PICACHO ON THE CALIFORNIA SIDE

THOUGH GOLD was first discovered on the Arizona side of the Colorado River at Gila City, mining activity was not restricted to the east side of the river in early days. Placer mining began around Picacho as early as 1861, and some mining has continued there to the present time. Successes were not always as spectacular as those across the river because of the low grade ore, but Picacho was the center of one of the largest mining enterprises on the Lower Colorado during the first decade of the Twentieth Century.

A local controversy exists concerning the identity of the individual who first struck gold at Picacho. The files of the Yuma County Historical Society contain a typescript which gives the credit to a man named Valenzuela. Mike Mendivil, a native of Picacho, thought that his grandfather, José Maria Mendivil, was the discoverer. A defunct periodical, *Calico Print*, gave the honor to a man named Pacheco in an article some years ago.

Lacking documentary evidence, it is impossible at this date to discover the truth. Mendivil seems a good choice for the honor. He lived at Picacho throughout the early days, and was deeply involved in most of the large mining ventures later.

There seems little doubt that the discovery was made in 1861, but there was probably no gold rush as a result. Gila City was still producing fair returns in its diggings, and the big La Paz rush started late that year. Picacho produced no fifty-five ounce chispas to match those being uncovered in the northern placers, but the boys who headed for La Paz may have been missing a good bet. Mike Mendivil says that the Pacheco family, who were placering at Picacho, often discarded pans of dirt worth five dollars. They refused to waste time washing anything worth less than twenty dollars.

The twenty dollar pans only lasted a short time, and the Mexicans working the washes in Picacho Basin gradually drifted away for more promising diggings. José Maria Mendivil left and went to work as a scout for the Union Army at Fort Yuma. When President Lincoln signed an act granting Arizona territorial status a few years later, he found more lucrative employment carrying the mail to the mining camps springing up on the east side of the river.[1]

Mendivil never forgot the gold he had washed from the Picacho sands. The idea came to him that the metal must have eroded from a vein in the hills around Picacho Basin. He had observed that most of it was found in washes south and east of Picacho Peak and reasoned that the source had to be near there. He began a methodical search of the area, and his diligence was rewarded when he located the Apache vein and several other outcroppings.[2]

It took a great deal of money to properly develop a hard rock mine, and Mendivil had very little. He filed claims on his discoveries and began working several with the assistance of relatives. They built a crude arrastra by the river and laboriously transported the ore for crushing. It was hard work and very inefficient.

J. S. Spann, a Yuma businessman, eventually heard of Mendivil's mine. He was invited to inspect it in the early Seventies, and liked what he saw. The businessman offered Mendivil a proposition. He and his business partner, a man named Poindexter, would form a corporation to work the Apache if Mendivil would deed the mine to them and accept a small cash payment with the balance of the sale price in company stock. When the offer was accepted, the partners purchased an old

[1]Mike Mendivil, "Gold, Guns, and Fiestas in Old Picacho," *Calico Print*, VII, No. 4 (February 1952), pp. 4-7.

[2]J. Wilson McKenney, "Saga of Old Picacho," *Desert Magazine*, II, 9 (March 1939), pp. 10-13.

five stamp mill that had been used upriver at the Buena Vista Mine and began the laborious task of moving it to Picacho. The cost was more than they had anticipated, and the pair were bankrupt before the stamps had crushed the first ton of ore.

Samuel Purdy, a Yuma politician, heard of Spann's predicament and interested some San Francisco investors in forming a company to take over the mine. The mill was soon crushing Apache ore, and Purdy waited expectantly for the profits to begin piling up. When the expected bonanza failed to materialize, he became disillusioned with mining and allowed the mine to be sold to satisfy creditors.[3]

Businessmen were a tenacious lot in those days, and another soon came forward to try his luck at running the Apache. David Neahr, a Yuma pioneer, took charge of the mine, convinced that he would be able to make it pay by using the skills he had acquired running a merchandising firm. He had the old stamp mill repaired, and it was soon processing ore which assayed as high as $28 a ton. Certain that a fortune was in the offing, he refused an offer of $150,000 for his Picacho properties and began constructing a larger mill with fifteen stamps.

The new mill caused Neahr a painful experience. He was supervising a work crew building an ore chute when a mule, hitched to a wagon loaded with lumber, was frightened by a sudden noise and bolted in his direction. Seeing the animal headed his way, Neahr managed to turn aside in time to escape the onrushing beast, but was struck by a piece of timber hanging from the wagon. It knocked him to the ground and one of the wagon wheels passed over his leg and broke it. Fortunately, the river steamer *Mohave* passed the mill shortly after the accident, and workmen hailed it. The captain obligingly transported the injured man to Yuma for treatment.

Louis J. F. Jaeger, a pioneer of the area, recorded the event in his diary in the following ungrammatical manner: "They brought W. D. Neaher in the afternoon from picho mind in steamer . . . god nerly kild yesterdy . . . a carte loded a hevy

[3]*Mining and Scientific Press*, March 8, 1878, p. 146.

Ruins of Neahr stamp mill at Picacho.

—*Frank Love Photo.*

stick . . . (2 words illegible) on carte and muel ran away an carte ran on W. D. Neaher & brok one lege & brused hiz musecles . . . I helpt to dress hiz wonds . . ."[4]

The mill was ready early in 1879. Neahr purchased a number of new ore wagons at a cost of $6,000 each to haul ore from the mines to his mill by the river, a distance of five miles. Things had never looked better for Picacho.

Since business interests in Yuma prevented Neahr from personally directing mining and milling, he turned the responsibility over to a trusted employee and sat back awaiting the profits. Production was good at the beginning, and returns ran as high as four or five hundred dollars a day in ore concentrates.

Success was too heady for the manager Neahr had put in charge of the mines. Wine, women, and song enticed him, and his female companions were able to coax him into spending company funds. When the deficit became so large it could no longer be hidden, the dishonest employee absconded with $7,000, and Neahr was forced into bankruptcy.[5]

Dr. DeWitt Jayne, a Troy, New York, drug manufacturer, was the next owner of the Picacho mines, but he did not seem very interested in getting them back into production. He seems to have regarded the mines as a good investment which would sell at a substantial profit at some future date. While waiting for some adventurous buyer to appear, the doctor contented himself with having the annual assessment work done, and filing for patents on the promising Venus, Mars, Goshen, and St. George claims.

Picacho experienced a hydraulic placer mining boom in the early Nineties, but the entire operation was tainted by fraud. This episode is described in the next chapter, "Promoters, Speculators, and Other Varmints."

The big decade in mining at Picacho, 1895-1905, resulted from the promotional antics of an ex-Senator, Stephen A.

[4]*Louis J. F. Jaeger Diary*, University of Arizona Library, p. 364.
[5]*Arizona Sentinel*, Dec. 30, 1893.

Dorsey, who masterminded a scheme which brought most of the claims in the area under control of the overcapitalized and ill-fated California King Gold Mines Company.

Dorsey, a native of Vermont, came of age at about the time the Civil War erupted. He enlisted in the Union Army and rose to the rank of Captain by war's end. Opportunity beckoned to Northerners with larcenous intent with the South a conquered and occupied country, and Dorsey joined the horde of carpetbaggers who headed for Dixie. Upon reaching Arkansas, the Vermont war veteran devised a plan to build a railroad in Central Arkansas, while bilking the state's taxpayers. *The Dictionary of American Biography* comments that the railroad company which Dorsey headed was "organized to defraud the state under the guise of giving state aid to railroads." An Arkansas newspaper complained that Dorsey "obtained state, county, and city aid, under the most solemn pledges. By trickery, hocus pocus, and legerdemain, the gauge of the road was changed from standard to narrow gauge."[6]

The promotion of the Arkansas Central Railroad gave Dorsey funds to buy a seat in Congress. Using his money to influence the legislature, he was able to obtain his election as United States Senator from Arkansas. When the Democratic Party regained control of the state governments in the South a few years later, Dorsey used his connections in Washington to get himself appointed as Secretary of the Republican National Committee.

His acquisition of high office had done little to quench Dorsey's instinct for shady deals. He was indicted along with several government officials in 1881 for conspiring to defraud the government of half a million dollars through fraudulent mail route contracts. Trial resulted in a hung jury and Dorsey escaped punishment, but charges were made later that the jury had been bribed. Nothing could be proven, and he departed from Washington undamaged except in reputation.

[6]"Stephen A. Dorsey," *Dictionary of American Biography*, ed. Allan Johnson and Dumas Malone, V (1950), p. 387.

The ex-Senator moved on to New Mexico, where it seemed that he was settling down as a gentleman farmer. The appearance was a deception. He was soon accused of being involved in a land fraud scheme. Again Dorsey escaped punishment and sought a more hospitable base of operations in Colorado.[7]

Dorsey appeared at Picacho in 1895, accompanied by several other men. He told the local miners and prospectors that he represented Denver capitalists who were interested in developing the area. Guided by the veteran miner, José Maria Mendivil, the party inspected a large number of claims, and purchased thirteen which bordered the mines owned by Dr. Jayne. Before departing for Denver, Dorsey took the residents of the Picacho area to Martinez's Store, where he bought out the entire stock. He told the miners and their families to "help themselves" to the merchandise, which was mostly whiskey, beer, cigars, and candy. They were no doubt impressed by the big spender from Colorado.

Rumors were soon flying that millionaires were buying up all of the claims at Picacho. A minor gold rush followed as every prospector for miles around tried to find an outcropping to peddle to the rich mine operators. Seventy-six new locations were recorded within the next few months. Some looked quite promising, and small mining companies were formed to operate them when they weren't bought by Dorsey. Typical of this development was the Gold Basin Mining and Milling Company which was incorporated in February 1896, with plans to mine eight claims which had been purchased by Judge C. B. Richards, owner of a smelter at Pueblo, Colorado. The new company capitalized their stock at one million dollars, and advertised that ore from their Maria de Oro vein would assay from $15 to $25 a ton.[8]

Dorsey kept the boom going when he announced that he would soon build a four and one-half mile railroad from his

[7]Ardie Poldervaart, "Black Robed Justice in New Mexico," *New Mexico Historical Review*, XXII, 4 (October 1947), pp. 386-387.

[8]*Engineering and Mining Journal*, Feb. 22, 1896, p. 188; Feb. 29, 1896, p. 212.

Old boiler at Dorsey's Mill, Picacho.

—*Frank Love Photo.*

mines to the river, and construct a twenty stamp mill. Further impetus was provided when he formed the Picacho Gold Mines Company in March 1896. Its board of directors contained several prominent names, including those of J. B. Grant, ex-Governor of Colorado; Samuel Morgan, a well-known Denver banker; William Teller, mining capitalist; and Henry Bolthoft, a millionaire mill builder. The firm had control of the numerous claims Dorsey had acquired.

Dorsey's original scheme must have been to gain control of all the mining claims in the Picacho area and sell the entire package to stock purchasers thousands of miles away. His Pichacho Gold Mines Company actually had very little capital, and the big names listed as directors must have been meant as bait to tempt investors. Taylor MacCleod, a long-time mining engineer, believed that was Dorsey's plan and had the courage to voice his warnings in the *Sentinel*. He said that "wild fantastic tales of 50-100 feet of $20-$50 per ton rock (at Picacho) are romances pure and simple." Most of the ore around Picacho was low grade rock worth about $5 a ton, he thought. He was afraid that novice investors were going to buy stock on the basis of such claims, and that they would go bankrupt and "curse . . . the gamble of mining when (they) had not used simple business discretion."

MacCleod's warnings got little publicity outside the Lower Colorado area, and Dorsey continued his promotional activities. It was rumored in the late summer of 1896 that he had purchased Dr. Jayne's mines for $220,000 with the backing of New York capital.[9] The tale was false, but it kept excitement at fever pitch at Picacho. Late in 1896, Dorsey traveled to London and sent back word that English investors were so impressed with possibilities at Picacho that they had advanced him funds to build a 100 stamp mill and begin construction on the railroad.[10] That report was also false. English investors had recently been swindled on a placer mining deal at Picacho, and

[9]*Arizona Sentinel*, Mar. 7, 1896; July 11, 1896; May 15, 1897.
[10]*Engineering and Mining Journal*, Nov. 21, 1896, p. 492.

Dorsey's glowing descriptions of mineral wealth awaiting the pick hardly enticed them to send more money to Picacho.

Dorsey's promotional efforts did have the effect of getting several new mining ventures launched. Fourteen small stamp mills were built in the next year or so at Picacho, and one company, the Golden Dream Mining Company, put 106 men to work on its claims. The owners had ignored Taylor MacCleod's warnings about low grade ore, and the old-timers were probably not surprised when the word got out that they were having financial difficulties less than a year after they had commenced mining.[11]

The town of Picacho came into existence during the flurry of activity in the mid-Nineties. José Mendivil patented much of the land around Picacho as a homestead. When it appeared that a mining boom was about to begin, he laid out a townsite along the river, which he recorded at the county seat on April 27, 1897. The town grew rapidly, and ninety children were soon enrolled in a school where Walter Ferguson and his wife, Emmaline, were the teachers.

Two saloons served the town. Billy Horan, the local constable, was the proprietor of the largest. Business must have been good at the drinking establishments. Mike Mendivil, who lived at Picacho as a boy, recalled in 1952 that one of the favorite sports of the younger set was watching the drunks stagger from the saloons.[12]

While Dorsey's big plans hadn't resulted in a single ton of ore production between 1895 and 1900, others were busy. Hiram Blaisdell bought Dr. Jayne's Venus Mine and put a crew to digging ore, which was transported to the old mill Neahr had built. The engineer installed a new type of roller mill in the building, which made the extraction process more efficient. He was soon employing seventy miners,[13] but the operation came to an abrupt halt in 1899 when the Jayne estate claimed they owned the mill site.

[11]*Yuma Sun*, July 23, 1897.
[12]Mendivil, *op. cit.*, pp. 4-7.
[13]*Yuma Sun*, Sept. 16, 1898.

Jayne's heirs said the doctor had acquired the mill site in 1885 from Neahr's estate. Joe Mendivil had sold it to Stephen Dorsey, thinking that it was a part of his homestead, and permitted Blaisdell to use it. Blaisdell decided to move his mill equipment to Kofa Mine, and halted his activities at Venus Mine while the matter was pending settlement.[14]

Full scale production got underway at Senator Mine, five miles south of Picacho, in April 1898. It is likely that the claim was dubbed "Senator" in honor of Dorsey. The ore vein had been discovered by Captain J. C. Beatty several years earlier, but he was unable to get financing until Dorsey's activities created outside interest. Beatty installed a twenty stamp mill with cyanide vats to treat the tailings, and began twenty-four hour operations. Low yields and a $4500 a month payroll forced him into bankruptcy within two months. A receiver was appointed and mining resumed, but it closed down again in June 1899, after John Gandolfo, a Yuma merchant, sued to collect a bill for lumber and supplies.[15]

Dorsey was busy with his schemes in the meantime. After participating in a controversial plan to resurrect the Harqua Hala mines, he had located financial support for his Picacho operation. Two former associates in the United States Senate, John P. Jones of Nevada and Richard Pettigrew of South Dakota, joined Dorsey and J. B. Landfield of New York in forming the California King Gold Mines Company. The organization took over the Picacho Gold Mines Company, and purchased Jayne's mines.[16]

Subsequent developments at Picacho strongly suggest that Dorsey, Landfield, and Jones conspired to bilk Pettigrew. The corporation began carrying out Dorsey's long-discussed plan for developing the mines. A 1000 ton reduction mill was built at the old millsite and work started on the railroad to carry ore from the mines. When completed, it was dubbed "The Picacho

[14]*Yuma Sun*, Jan. 27, 1899; *Arizona Sentinel*, Jan. 28, 1899.

[15]*Arizona Sentinel*, Apr. 2, 1898; May 28, 1898; June 3, 1899.

[16]*Arizona Sentinel*, May 1, 1901; May 10, 1901; Apr. 30, 1902; *Yuma Sun*, Dec. 14, 1900.

Remains of Senator Dorsey's Picacho Mill, 1972.

—*Frank Love Photo.*

and Colorado River Railroad." Just as real mining was about to begin, Dorsey and Landfield sold their entire interest in the corporation to Pettigrew. Evidence is lacking that Jones sold out at the same time, but his close relationship with Dorsey in a shady stock promotion in New York City a year earlier suggests that he was a confederate in the conspiracy.

The pair had been instrumental in promoting the Tripler Liquid Air Corporation, which advertised that it intended to exploit the inventions of Charles E. Tripler, a New York inventor. The corporation took advantage of Arizona's easy laws and capitalized itself for $10,000,000. When a massive advertising campaign created a good market for the company stock, Jones and Dorsey quietly sold the $1,000,000 in stock they had assigned to themselves as promoters. The entire affair came to light only when a disgruntled stock purchaser, Israel Goldberg, made a complaint to the New York Police Department that he had been cheated. An investigation of the matter led to bankruptcy for the firm, but all charges against Jones and Dorsey had to be dropped. They had done nothing illegal.[17]

Dorsey's sale of his interests to Pettigrew made him wealthy. He promptly took a wife, Miss Laura Bigelow, and following a society wedding at Grace Church in New York City, set out to see Europe with his bride. He informed reporters that he "no longer felt it necessary to overwork himself to keep the wolf a safe distance from the door."[18]

California King was almost immediately in financial difficulties, which led Allen Smith, one of the stockholders, to complain that the management was incompetent. He said that Pettigrew had dismissed a competent superintendent, Emerson Gee, and replaced him with a machinist who was not capable of managing the operation. Production had fallen by fifty per cent, he complained.

[17]*New York Times*, Aug. 29, 1901; Aug. 30, 1901, Sept. 12, 1901; *Arizona Republican*, Dec. 3, 1901.

[18]*Arizona Sentinel*, July 9, 1902; Oct. 8, 1902.

Smith told the *Los Angeles Mining Review* that the July 1903 cleanup was worth $26,500, but California King had only shipped $16,116 in bullion that month. He announced that he intended to hire a Pinkerton detective to determine what had become of the missing $10,000. His queries to the New York office only brought evasions.

The miners at Picacho may have been partly responsible for the eventual failure of the California King operation. Smith alleged that they were bragging "that their wages cut no figure, as they steal so much gold out of the mines and sell it to the saloon keepers."[19] He was probably correct. Mike Mendivil has written that Picacho miners were notorious high graders. "They'd put the stuff in their shoes and socks—and they'd bring it out in sandwiches. Yes, golden sandwiches . . . they had these tacos, they call them nowadays. When the inspector asked them what they had, they'd say, 'You see, that's part of my lunch I didn't eat.' "[20]

California King's huge payroll for 700 men made Picacho a lively town. Like most other mining camps, it had its share of gunfights and killings. The most sensational occurred in April 1903, and resulted in the death of a miner, Santiago Lopez, and a hated deputy law officer, Pete Burke. The lawman had built a fearsome reputation at Fortuna and other camps along the Colorado, and had six notches in his gun as proof. The consensus of local opinion was that he often killed "without justification."

Burke had become especially obnoxious while serving as Billy Horan's deputy at Picacho. He kept a paper in his pocket containing a list of names and bragged to the miners that he meant to legally kill everyone on the list. "They'll all go," he said.[21]

Burke's trigger-happy attitude was the indirect cause of his death. Billy Horan, Picacho's saloon-owning constable, was

[19]*Arizona Sentinel*, Sept. 16, 1903, quoting the *Los Angeles Mining Review*, n.d.
[20]Mendivil, *op. cit.*, pp. 4-7.
[21]Mendivil, *op. cit.*, pp. 4-7. He calls the deputy "Bohorkus," but other details match the *Sentinel* account.

cleaning his gun in his drinking establishment when it accidentally discharged. The bullet went harmlessly through the ceiling, but Burke who had been standing outside rushed in, recklessly firing his gun. The deputy assumed a gunfight was in progress. One of the wild shots went through a wall and killed Santiago Lopez.

Horan placed Burke under arrest in order to protect him from a group of Mexican miners, who were enraged over the senseless death of Lopez. When mine superintendent Ridgeway arrived on the scene minutes later, Horan deputized him to assist in transporting Burke out of Picacho to the custody of a justice of the peace. As the law officers were attempting to place Burke in a wagon, a large crowd gathered and threatened to seize the prisoner and lynch him.

Matters came to a head when a brother of the dead miner suddenly stepped from the mob and advanced on Burke with a drawn pistol. "For God's sake, don't kill me," the deputy whined. The Lopez brother paid no attention to his pleas and fired, hitting the prisoner in the shoulder.

Convinced that he was about to be lynched, Burke jumped from the wagon and ran toward a clump of brush some distance away. Twenty or more of the crowd drew their guns and began firing at him with no luck. When it appeared that the fleeing man might escape, one of the mob, Raphael Belarde, set out in pursuit, firing as he ran. One of Belarde's shots hit Burke in the head and killed him.

Ridgeway, the deputized mine superintendent, had attempted to halt the mob when they opened fire on Burke. Someone shot him in the leg during the melee.

Immediately after the shooting, Belarde and Lopez fled into the desert. San Diego County offered a $250 reward for the capture of Belarde, and the governor doubled the ante to $500. Lopez reached Mexico and was never captured, but San Bernardino law officers caught up with Belarde at Aqua Mansa several months later.

Ore chutes at Neahr Mill, Picacho.

—*Frank Love Photo.*

The authorities planned to return Belarde to Picacho for trial, but reconsidered after Horan wired them. He suggested trial be held elsewhere "owing to the superior number of Mexicans, all friendly to the man . . . (who) would not hesitate to rescue and set him free." When Belarde was sent to San Diego for trial, Horan told the *Sentinel* that he was "much relieved." The accused murderer was found guilty and sentenced to serve a three year term in prison.

California King's financial difficulties surfaced in February 1904, when they were forced to borrow $200,000 from the North American Trust Company to continue operations. A property mortgage secured the loan. An immediate solution seemed to be to lower operating costs and company officials set about doing it. One economy measure involved levying a charge of $2.00 a week for water that had previously been provided without charge to the miners' families. When this was attempted in June 1904, the company found themselves facing a strike. One hundred and fifty of the miners gathered in Horan's Saloon and vowed that they would not return to work until the water charge was withdrawn. The company gave in after a day, and the men returned to work, but hindsight suggests that the miners might have been wise to accept the fee. The company was unable to survive the next crisis.

An accident closed the California King forever. When a governor belt broke on a piece of machinery in July 1904, it released a twenty-ton flywheel which sailed through the roof of the mill and landed one half mile away in pieces. In the face of a $40,000 judgment which they had lost to the Colorado Iron Works in the courts several months earlier, the owners were unable to raise money to repair the damaged machinery. Company property had to be sold to satisfy debtors.

The last act began at Picacho when José Mendivil and Allen Smith, two former California King stockholders, joined with Captain Isaac Polhamus, an old-time steamer operator, to form the California Queen Mining Company.[22] The new firm built

[22]*Arizona Sentinel*, Apr. 15, 1903; June 10, 1903; June 24, 1903; Dec. 16, 1903; May 1, 1905.

a 100 ton mill at the mines, intending to save the cost of transporting ore five miles to the river for reduction, but rising costs doomed their enterprise. The construction of Laguna Dam downstream from Picacho ended forever the transportation of ore concentrates by steamer, and it was necessary to ship their product by wagon to the railroad. With gradually declining ore values, and increased costs, the company collapsed.

Several small mining companies have carried out operations in and near Picacho since the early 1900s, but none of them have amounted to much. Very little of old Picacho remains today. Ruins of the old mill by the river are still quite visible, and the piles of white tailings stand out as reminders of the glory days. Much of the town was covered by backwater from Laguna Dam when it was completed. Visitors these days probably doubt that Picacho ever claimed 2,500 inhabitants.

CHAPTER SIX

PROMOTERS, SPECULATORS, AND OTHER VARMINTS

"Definitions: *A bonanza—a hole in the ground owned
by a damned liar.*"[1]

MINING has its "get rich quick" aspects and has always attracted a number of persons who stay barely within the limits of the law. It also attracted more than its fair share of outright swindlers. The mining fraternity along the Lower Colorado may have been no worse than their brethren elsewhere, but history records that it contained a goodly sprinkling of cheaters.

Bunco artists began plying their trade early in the region. The first recorded swindle may have been the one described by the *San Diego Union* in 1864. Several con men turned up in La Paz with pieces of coal they said they had dug from a mine at Castle Dome. They commenced selling shares in Arizona's first coal mine, and left town with $60 in profits. It took the coal mine stockholders several months to discover that the coal had really come from a fuel pile at Fort Yuma.[2]

No one along the Lower Colorado seems to have been victimized by the great diamond swindle of 1872, but the affair did create some excitement for a while and caused some red faces later. The clever hoax was devised by a slick promoter, Asbury Harpending, and two confederates, Arnold and Slack. After carefully seeding a remote area in Wyoming with gems purchased in Europe, they sold shares in their diamond field to a

[1]*Anglo-Colorado Mining Guide*, July 30, 1904, p. 4.
[2]*San Diego Union*, Apr. 14, 1864; *Bancroft's Arizona Scraps*, Vol. II, p. 326.

number of prominent Americans. In order to prevent the salted mines from being examined, the trio put out the story that the real location of the field was Arizona. A geologist, Clarence King, eventually located their salted mines and exposed the swindle after finding one diamond atop of a rock. Until the truth was known, Arizonians had a merry time hunting for diamonds. The *Sentinel* reported in August 1872 that "many of our good citizens can be seen early in the morning and late in the afternoon, on the hills surrounding our town, searching for precious stones." District Judge DeForest Porter and a member of the local bar, Clarence Gray, picked up two rocks they believed to be small diamonds. When a man named Baker offered to buy one for $500, the wary jurist refused his offer.

A few weeks later, a diamond hunting expedition departed secretly from Yuma. Among its members were the sharp-eyed judge and Julius Seibeck, a local miner who called himself "Professor." The newspaper reported a week later that "The diamond expedition which left here last week, having met with a misfortune, returned a few days ago." What the misfortune was the *Sentinel* never said. Perhaps a scarcity of diamonds might have been the problem.

It took a large amount of capital to properly develop a gold or silver mine; more than the usual prospector was likely to have. This led to the practice of selling claims to mining promoters who would form a corporation, sell stock to raise development funds, and hire a superintendent to operate the mine. Since prospectors were not a bit hesitant to exaggerate the richness of their claims and produce only the best ore for assaying, such ventures were a real gamble.

One problem frequently encountered by those who engaged in mine promotion was that capital ran out before the mine could begin producing ore in paying quantities. This dilemma was handled by having the company trustees vote an "assessment" on each share of stock to raise additional money. If the stock owner refused to ante up the additional cash, the trustees might legally sell enough shares owned by the non-paying stockholder to cover the cost of his assessment. It was a fair arrangement only when the promoters were honest.

Dishonest promoters used the arrangement to bilk the naive or ignorant. They would buy a worthless prospect for a few dollars and advertise it as if it were a newly discovered Comstock Lode. Having disposed of a number of shares, the promoters would elect themselves and their cronies to the board of directors, spend the development moneys, and levy assessments on all who had been foolish enough to buy the stock. When stockholders soured on the deal, they bought a new mine, formed a new corporation, and began to exploit a new crop of suckers. Stephen Dorsey, the Picacho promoter who operated in similar fashion, formed three different mining corporations in 1904 and 1905 after he had gotten out of the Picacho operations.

One of the slickest operators in the Lower Colorado region was O. A. Pease, who dealt in mines around Quartzsite and Salome. Pease located some claims in 1905 and put out the story that he had suddenly discovered them to be bonanzas. He said that a neighbor made him aware of the value of his mines after getting permission to quarry some rock from one of the claims to build a house. The home builder took a piece of quartz from the mine and discovered that it contained gold. A closer examination disclosed that the quartz assayed at $50 a ton.

Pease said that when the neighbor informed him his claim was a rich gold mine, he formed the Amalgamated Gold Mines Company. He told the story of his fabulous mine to H. J. Beemer, a New York millionaire, and convinced the easterner he should buy into the corporation for $2,500,000. Pease told Beemer that he would only have to ante up $375,000 in cash, and might pay the remainder of the purchase price from his share of the profits. An attorney with whom Pease was acquainted, S. S. Parks of Chicago, willingly acted as a legal advisor to Beemer during the sale, and accepted a seat on the board of directors. Pease helped Beemer find a "mine expert," who examined the claims and pronounced them worth a fortune.

Beemer was soon crying, "Fraud!" He charged that the mine expert had deliberately given him a false report and that the helpful lawyer was in reality a partner of Pease's. He had been "gold bricked," he said. Pease showed him ore samples from a mine other than the one he had bought. In addition, Beemer claimed, Pease padded the company payroll and used company employees to work on personal claims which did not belong to the Amalgamated Gold Mines Corporation. He filed a civil suit to recover damages.

Pease struck back by having Amalgamated declared bankrupt. A sympathetic judge saw nothing unfair in appointing Solomon Pease, a brother of O. A. Pease, receiver.

The strategy backfired. When the receiver went to take possession of the property, workers at the mine who sympathized with Beemer refused to let him take possession. That forced the receiver to return to court to demand a contempt citation against the persons occupying the property, and Beemer's supporters used the occasion to remind the judge that Solomon Pease was the brother of the accused swindler. The jurist wisely refused to take action on the contempt demands.

Beemer wasn't satisfied to let the matter rest, and charged Pease with embezzlement. He was brought before Judge J. P. Redondo of Yuma for trial, but the jurist decided there was insufficient evidence to warrant holding him. Insult was added to Beemer's sense of injury shortly afterward when a jury awarded him $1.00 in damages in his civil suit against the promoter.[3]

Some promoters went farther than New York to locate suckers. England seemed to produce an especially gullible type of mine investor who was eager to squander his money recklessly on mines in the Southwest. Raymond Rossiter, editor of a mining periodical, observed in 1881 that "Of all the large

[3]*Arizona Sentinel*, Aug. 31, Sept. 21, 1872; June 28, Sept. 13, 1905; Feb. 21, Apr. 25, 1906.

class of idiotic capitalists, the Britisher shows the least symptom of intelligence."[4] The history of the ill-fated Picacho Gold Mining Company suggests Rossiter was right.

L. C. Moreland, an experienced hydraulic miner, discovered the placer deposits at Picacho. He contacted two promoters, Allen J. Smith of Oakdale, California, and Clayton Smith, an Englishman. The three began concocting plans for an ill-conceived hydraulic placering operation that *Mining and Scientific Press* described as "one of the most absurd engineering feats ever undertaken in the west."[5] They planned to pump water from the river into a three thousand gallon tank five hundred feet above the river. By using three pumps, they hoped to force water five miles through a twelve inch pipeline and have it reach the mine site with enough pressure to wash out the gold.

Such a scheme required money, and they had none. Clayton Smith, the English partner, explained their plans to Baron Grant, a wily English stock promoter. Grant had promoted the infamous Emma Mine in Utah two decades earlier, that had resulted in cries of "fraud" heard as far away as the White House in Washington. The Englishman agreed to give their project his full attention.

A corporation was needed, and the trio promptly formed the Picacho Gold Mining Company. Clayton Smith assumed the office of president, with Allen Smith acting as superintendent. Moreland accepted the post of general manager. It must be assumed all three voted themselves handsome salaries.

With the technical details out of the way, Baron Grant got busy with the task of selling the company's stock. He unloaded a million dollars worth in short order and made a personal profit of $600,000 in the transaction. Much of the stock was purchased by a gullible soap manufacturer, R. W. Hudson of Liverpool.[6]

[4]*Engineering and Mining Journal*, July 23, 1881, p. 53.
[5]*Arizona Sentinel*, Feb. 16, 1895, quoting *Mining and Scientific Press*, n.d.
[6]*Arizona Sentinel*, Feb. 2, Feb. 16, 1895.

By September 1893, the pumps, storage tank, and pipeline had been completed at a cost of $200,000 and the grand experiment began. To the dismay of Moreland and the Smiths, the expensive equipment would hardly lift water from the river to the storage tank and, when it reached the mine after its five mile trip, it hardly had enough pressure to flow from the pipe. The operators quickly informed the local newspapers that the pumps had broken down, but assured the media that they had been washing gold from the desert sands at profits that ran from $100 to $500 a day before breaking down. Moreland demonstrated his faith in the project by selling his shares to Fred Baker, owner of an iron works in Los Angeles.

The failure of the firm to send dividends to the stockholders in England soon brought visitors. A. W. Toppe and C. G. W. Locke of London arrived in Yuma in March 1894, to make an on the spot investigation of the corporation. Their findings caused them to summon Thomas I. Birch of London, one of the stockholders, and Hudson, the soap manufacturer. They arrived on the scene on April 23 after Toppe and Locke had traveled to New York to meet them and escort them to the mine. Birch made a big hit in Yuma by denouncing Americans and thanking God that he was an Englishman as he stepped from the train.[7]

The English stockholders soon convinced themselves they had been duped, but thought they might be able to salvage something by ridding themselves of the two Smiths, whom they denounced as swindlers. The Yuma *Times* published their accusations, but found themselves named in a $50,000 libel suit. When the case came to trial before Yuma Third District Court on April 2, 1895, the Smiths failed to show up to prove they had been unjustly accused, and the matter was dismissed with the Smiths paying court costs.[8]

The English owners hired a new superintendent, and gave the operation another try later that year. They were soon con-

[7]*Ibid.*, Feb. 2, Mar. 3, Apr. 28, 1894.
[8]*Arizona Sentinel*, Oct. 6, 1894; Apr. 27, 1895.

vinced that the venture was foolishness, and gave it up. It was costing them $132 a day just to provide enough wood to fuel the steam boilers that powered the pumps. They managed to recoup a small part of their losses by selling the equipment to Stephen Dorsey, who was just beginning his grandiose mining scheme at Picacho.

Most promoters were not able to find free-spending millionaires like Beemer or Hudson to purchase their stocks, and had to content themselves bilking the small investor. A typical promotion of this type was the Arizona Giant Copper Company. Four Los Angeles sharpies, Thomas Blakely, Melvin R. Gay, N. G. Douglas, and Henry L. Adams formed the corporation in 1901 after buying some old mining claims ten miles southeast of Ehrenberg, the Self Defense Group. The mines had been worked for gold years earlier, and contained some low grade copper deposits.

A high-powered advertising campaign in California was soon trumpeting Arizona Giant stock as the investor's dream, a can't fail proposition. For $.50 a share, the lucky buyer not only purchased shares in the valuable copper mines, but was also presented with a guarantee that he would receive his original investment back within ten years. A special bargain offer was made to thrifty souls who needed no such assurance. They might buy the same stock for $.25 a share.[9]

It seems that some investors paid more than the advertised price. A Redlands, California woman, Mrs. Grace Steel, took Arizona Giant to court in 1903 asserting that Blakely and Adams had sold her shares for $1.00 each. She was quite angry when she discovered later that they were actually worth five cents.

With the true worth of their copper corporation exposed in public, the promoters decided to take their profits and run. Blakely and Gay filed suit against the corporation on grounds that they had not received the salaries they voted themselves. It was all legally correct and the court could do nothing but

[9]*Yuma Sun*, Jan. 11, 1901.

Arizona's easy laws for incorporation brought ads like this and encouraged dishonest promoters. (1906.)

—*Los Angeles Mining Review.*

declare Arizona Giant bankrupt. When the mines were sold at public auction to satisfy the promoter's demands, Gay and Blakely bought them for the amount of the judgment they had been granted by the courts. A few months later they sold the same mines to the Arizona Prince Mining Company.[10]

Not all promoters were as clever as the founders of the Arizona Giant. Some devised mining schemes that bordered on the ridiculous, but they were still able to find backers with money to squander. Professor Howland, the San Francisco divining rod miner, fits this category. Howland first appeared along the Lower Colorado in 1893 and laid claim to several placer locations two miles south of Mohawk Station on the Southern Pacific Railroad.

The professor went to San Francisco shortly afterward and proceeded to tell prospective investors that he had used his divining rod to locate the ancient bed of the Colorado River. "Placer gold will be found in great quantities when we dig down to bedrock," he told his gullible listeners. It was not too difficult to find believers, and the professor was back at Mohawk by November 1894, digging away at what he said was the bed of the Colorado. He had a large crew working around the clock, and told the curious that he expected to find "buried untold wealth" at any minute.

The gold was elusive, and Howland was forced to return to San Francisco a few months later to replenish his supply of capital. Surprisingly, he still was able to find backers, and returned to Mohawk in April 1895. He commenced digging again for his hidden bonanza.[11] No one seemed to mind the insane promotion along the Lower Colorado because it provided employment for some people and the professor paid good wages. There is no record that he ever found any gold. Perhaps his divining rod was faulty.

Divining rods found believers among the mining fraternity as well as with the investors. John McCasey, assayer in the

[10]*Arizona Sentinel*, Mar. 4, Oct. 28, 1903; Feb. 15, July 12, 1905.
[11]*Ibid.*, Nov. 17, 1894; Apr. 13, 1895.

Harqua Hala area, told of being impressed by a "hoodoo stick" operator in that camp in 1892. He said the man with the divining rod was named James and that he hailed from Lodi, California. In a demonstration of his skills for the miners, McCasey swore that the rod dipped every time it passed over the Golden Chariot ore vein. The assayer admitted he was impressed by the performance but told the *Sentinel* that "I do not believe that anything but muscles and tools . . . will reveal the existence of precious metals in quantity."[12] He was probably right. The Golden Chariot never became much of an ore producer.

The bizarre career of Professor Giles Otis Pearce must certainly be the most fantastic true tale of promotions along the Lower Colorado. Pearce, who was said to be an English mine expert, first appeared in the area in 1897, where he busied himself examining the mining claims of Taylor MacCleod in the old Weaver District north of Yuma. Shortly afterward, it was announced that the Rio Colorado Gold Extraction Company of Colorado City, Colorado, had bonded MacCleod's claims and would erect a stamp mill on the site. The professor proclaimed the mines valuable and found backers to operate them.

He may have been correct in his judgment that the mines were worthwhile, but the decision to build a mill was an error. There was not sufficient water in the area, and the mill could only operate part of the day. But that was not a concern for Pearce. He had withdrawn from the corporation and sued the other stockholders for $22,500 on grounds that they had wrongfully sold a large block of company stock. A second suit was entered to collect back wages of $250, and the court granted him a judgment in that matter.[13]

While Pearce's larger lawsuit was still pending, the Yuma *Sun* spotted an editorial in the *Denver Mining Reporter* concerning the professor's earlier activities in Colorado. The local paper copied the item for the edification of its readers. It ap-

[12]*Ibid.*, July 2, 1892.
[13]*Yuma Sun*, Jan. 14, Apr. 22, 1898.

peared as follows: "Giles Otis Pearce, known in Colorado Springs as a half-crazy, so-called metallurgist, with impossible schemes, together with being the originator of the Pike's Peak Tunnel Project, is out with a patent for extracting gold from sea water. As the fool crop is continually getting ripe, he will probably gather in some of them with it."[14]

Caught between the lawsuits instituted by Pearce, and insufficient water to run their mill, the Rio Colorado Gold Extraction Company was forced into bankruptcy. It was sold at sheriff's auction to Gandolfo and Sanguinetti, a Yuma mercantile firm. A year passed and the professor was nearly forgotten.

Suddenly he was in the news again. Pearce, who had moved to Santa Ana, California, was having wife trouble. After becoming disenchanted with her husband, Mrs. Pearce departed from the family home and boarded a train to Los Angeles. The professor somehow learned of his wife's departure and was able to board the same train in an attempt to stop her. He convinced a helpful passenger that his estranged wife was really a lunatic who needed forcible restraint. The two tied her up and sent a telegram to the Los Angeles Police Department requesting assistance with an insane woman they had in tow.

The police met the train as requested, but they came to the conclusion, after talking to Mrs. Pearce, that she was not mentally unbalanced. Much to the professor's dismay, the police untied her and let her go. Pearce proceeded to the station house and demanded that the officers issue a warrant for his spouse's arrest. They refused and locked him up instead.

His jail term must have been short because Pearce began promoting a mining firm known as the United Mines Mining Company two months later. When the Yuma *Sun* learned of the professor's latest scheme, they sent a telegram to the *Denver Mining Reporter* describing it and requesting an evaluation of the company. The reply was short and to the point. "This is an out and out fraud. The manager is well-known in

[14]*Ibid.*, Aug. 12, 1898, quoting *Denver Mining Reporter*, n.d.

Colorado. There is not the slightest chance that any money invested in the company will ever come back to the investor."[15]

The same could have been said of many of the so-called mining corporations along the Lower Colorado.

[15]*Ibid.*, Nov. 17, 1899; Oct. 12, Dec. 28, 1900.

CHAPTER SEVEN

SILVER BONANZAS

MOST OF the silver produced along the Lower Colorado has come from a small area north of Yuma. Miners appropriately named it "Silver District" many years ago. Four important mines were in the region: the Black Rock, the Pacific, the Clip or James G. Blaine, and the Red Cloud. Other claims held out bright promises for a time, but proved disappointing in the end.

Jacob Snively, discoverer of the Castle Dome mines, was the first to locate silver in the Trigos Mountains. He was looking for gold in 1863, but found several outcroppings of argentiferous galena, a silver-lead ore.[1] He filed claims, but thought little of their worth and drifted on southeast into the Castle Dome Range. He found galena there which he thought more valuable, and the Castle Dome District was soon booming. The deposits in the Trigos were forgotten.

Fifteen years passed with the Trigos untouched by miners. In late winter, 1877, George Norton of Yuma grubstaked Walter Millar, Neil Johnson, and Gus Crawford to do some prospecting.[2] All three located claims in the Trigos, but Johnson's turned out to be the best. His Black Rock and Pacific mines became early producers.

As often was the case, the discoverer realized little from his strike. Johnson made the mistake of going on a spree a few weeks after his strike. While drinking in Thomas Hughes's Yuma saloon, he began bragging about his rich claims. Hughes,

[1]*Mining and Scientific Press*, Mar. 2, 1878, p. 133.
[2]*Arizona Sentinel*, Aug. 17, 1895.

who had been drinking with him, asked how much he would take for them. When Johnson replied that he would accept three hundred dollars, the saloon owner bought them in a moment of drunken generosity.

Things looked different to Hughes when he sobered up the next day, and he went looking for Johnson, hoping to get his money back. He found him, but Johnson had spent the money and told him he would have to keep the mines.

Hughes took a trip to Silver District several weeks later to see what he had bought. He returned convinced that he had a true bonanza, and began telling everyone who was willing to listen. His word-of-mouth advertising paid off in 1881 when a Boston firm bought the two claims for $150,000. Hughes purchased a home in Los Angeles, turned over $40,000 to his wife, and set out to see the sights of New York City. His wife never heard from him again. She used her capital to enter the real estate business and became moderately wealthy.

News of the strike brought other prospectors. Warren Hammond, Charles Burnham, and George Rowher arrived in Yuma without a penny in 1878. Hammond got a grubstake by pawning his shotgun. After a few days of prospecting, Hammond located the Red Cloud claim, which produced silver longer than any other mine in the district. He took a half interest as its discoverer and gave a quarter each to his partners, Rowher and Burnham.[3] By then the rush was on and the Yuma County recorder's office was soon flooded with claims. Eighty-one were filed in one month during 1879.

Silver District was legally organized at a miner's meeting on January 20, 1879. Hammond, the Red Cloud discoverer, chaired the meeting and the miners selected Walter Millar to be the official claims recorder. Among the resolutions they passed was one which excluded "Chinamen," and another which forbade the sale of liquor at the mines. They did agree to allow the sale of alcoholic beverages at Norton's Landing near the river.[4]

[3]*Ibid.*, Aug. 24, 1895.
[4]*Ibid.*, Jan. 25, 1879.

The district may have been unique in one respect. It could boast a lady miner. Mrs. Dobson, a Solano (California) widow came to the region after operating a quicksilver mine that her husband had located in California. After his death, she mined the claim, with the assistance of a twelve-year-old son. News of the strikes in Silver District led her to abandon it and begin prospecting in Silver District. Her luck was poor, but her persistence led the miners to give her a claim. They told the *Sentinel* that they were awarding her the Silver City claim "in recognition of her grit."[5] There is no record that the Silver City was a bonanza, and the widow gave up mining to run a boarding house for miners at Norton's Landing.

The Black Rock, Pacific, and Red Cloud were all within a few miles of one another, and a crude town began to develop between them. Residents called it Pacific City and drew up a petition requesting a post office. After the post office was acquired, they managed to get stage service to Yuma and Ehrenberg on a tri-weekly basis.

In spite of the fact that liquor sales had been outlawed at the mines, drinking caused the town's first shooting scrape in May 1880. Jesus Osuna, one of the miners, went on a spree of several day's duration and became mean and antagonistic. While inebriated, he went to the home of a married step-daughter who was ill. When he tried to crawl into bed with the sick woman, relatives intervened and forced him to leave the house.

When several miners attempted to shame Osuna for his behavior, he pulled his pistol and fired two shots at one of his critics, Juan Martinez. He missed his mark, and Martinez drew a gun and returned the fire. So did José Valenzuela! One of their shots hit Osuna, and he fell dead. Everyone agreed Valenzuela and Martinez acted from self-defense, and the matter was dropped.[6]

Good reports on the Silver District mines attracted outside attention in 1879. Julius Siebeck, a colorful graduate of the Freiberg School of Mines, in Germany, was mainly respon-

[5]*Ibid.*, Feb. 15, 1879.
[6]*Ibid.*, May 15, 1880.

sible. When Siebeck reported to the Prescott newspaper that the silver ore in the district was a true bonanza, it came to the attention of the territorial governor, John Charles Fremont. Prescott was the territorial capital at that time, and the "Pathfinder of the West" had just taken office after being appointed by President Hayes.

Fremont had lost a fortune in railroad speculation, but hoped to recoup his losses by selling Arizona mining properties while drawing a salary as governor. Judge Charles Silent, an associate justice of the Arizona Supreme Court, and several attorneys, were cooperating with him. Silent and Fremont were making plans to sell Arizona mines on the East Coast at the time they read of the strike in Silver District.

The governor and the judge left for the east early in the summer of 1879. The official purpose of their trip was to prevent the resettlement of the Pima Indian tribe from the Casa Grande Valley to the Salt River Valley, which was beginning to bloom as an irrigated garden spot.[7] By using the governor's extensive political connections to good advantage, they were able to persuade the government to reverse its decision, and they moved on to New York, where they were soon reported to be "making barrels of money back east selling mines."[8]

When Red Cloud Mine was sold shortly after the Fremont-Silent trip, the miners in Silver District believed the judge responsible and changed the name of their camp from Pacific City to Silent.[9] It seems likely that the judge was only a front man for Fremont, whose policy was to keep his name out of mining deals.[10]

[7]Bert M. Fireman, "Fremont's Arizona Adventure," *The American West*, I, 1 (Winter 1964), p. 14.

[8]*The Daily Miner*, June 10, 1879.

[9]This is an educated guess. In May 1880, the *Sentinel* was still referring to it as Pacific City. News that the mine had been sold appeared on May 22, 1880. By October 23, 1880, *Mining and Scientific Press* was referring to the Red Cloud and Silent Mine, and on November 18, 1880, the *Sentinel* reported that the post office at Norton's Landing would be named Silent Post Office.

[10]Fireman, *op. cit.*, p. 15.

Much circumstantial evidence points to Fremont as the promoter of Silver District rather than to the jurist. The governor wrote to a business associate from New York on July 31, 1879, that "Messrs. John Hoey and J. C. Babcock of the Adams Express Company for themselves and friends . . . have executed a contract with me for the sale of some twenty mines, the contract to depend on the report of experts sent out by the two parties, Professor Maynard on the part of Adams Express people and Dr. Einhorn . . ."[11] Maynard appeared in Yuma to inspect the Red Cloud in October and told the *Sentinel* it fully met his expectations. A second expert, J. D. Wilson, appeared in Silver District two months later and said he was also impressed. Perhaps it was only coincidence, but Maynard was a house guest at Silent's Tucson home while Wilson was inspecting the mines.

Strange business transactions occurred almost immediately after the two experts completed their inspections. Rumors began to circulate that the Red Cloud had been sold, but no one knew who had purchased it. Then it was disclosed that the buyer was the Iron Cap Mining Company, a nearly bankrupt firm which owned several Silver District claims. Iron Cap had been in such precarious financial straits a month earlier that they had levied an assessment on shareholders of $1.50 per share to continue operations. Within a month, some great miracle had come to pass. Not only was the company able to buy the Red Cloud for $100,000, but they also informed their stockholders that the financial crisis had passed and the $1.50 assessment was cancelled.[12] The mystery deepened in May when Iron Cap abruptly sold the mine to the New Yorkers, who had dispatched Maynard and Wilson to Arizona.

What was the explanation for Iron Cap's sudden affluence? No rich silver vein had been tapped on company property. The answer probably lies buried with Governor Fremont and Judge Silent. One might theorize that either Maynard or Wilson

[11]Letter from John Fremont to Rogers, New York, July 31, 1879, Bancroft Library, CB 392-2.
[12]*Arizona Sentinel*, Nov. 1, Dec. 27, 1879; Feb. 21, Apr. 3, 1880.

Judge Charles Silent.

—Courtesy Dept. of Library and Archives, Phoenix, Arizona.

tipped them off that they would report favorably on the Red Cloud and recommend its purchase. Fremont and Silent probably used the financially distressed Iron Cap firm to hide their own purchase of the mine. It appeared to the public that Iron Cap had bought and sold the mine, but Fremont and Silent were probably the real buyers and sellers.

There is no direct proof of this theory, but there is abundant evidence that contemporaries thought Fremont and Silent capable of such practices. So strongly suspicious of the pair was Arizona Territory's delegate to Congress that he preferred charges against Judge Silent in April 1880. Delegate Campbell told Congress that Silent and Fremont had been buying, selling, and bonding mines that were within the jurisdiction of the judge's court and, in some instances, involved in litigation before his court. He also alleged that the jurist was drawing three salaries as the result of a bill lobbied through the territorial legislature by Fremont's cronies. The Republican Attorney General, Devens, investigated the charges and concluded that they were politically motivated, since Campbell was a Democrat.[13] In spite of his receiving an acquittal, Silent resigned his judicial post a few months later. It is possible Silent offered to resign in return for exoneration.

Silver District soon found that the New York buyers meant business. They dispatched a steamer upriver laden with a twenty-five ton smelter and made contracts with Jesus Contreras and Joe Redondo to transport ore, wood, and charcoal to their furnace. They had the smelter in operation and a work force of nearly a hundred mining Red Cloud galena by early 1881.

Word was out shortly afterward that Red Cloud was in financial difficulty. Creditors attached a shipment of bullion enroute to San Francisco. Mining was halted in July 1881, and S. S. Draper, the mine superintendent who had been sent out from New York, was fired. Charles Knapp of Deposit, New York,

[13]*Arizona Sentinel*, June 26, 1880.

replaced Draper. Though Knapp was one of the owners, he had no more luck than his predecessor. Mounting bills led creditors to force the sale of the mine at sheriff's auction in October 1882. The Deposit, New York, bank which had loaned money for the purchase of the mine, made the highest bid and became the Red Cloud owner.

The bank made no effort to operate the mine for the next several years. Inactivity on the part of its owners led William Werninger, a Yuma politician and miner, to try to jump the claim in 1885. Julius Siebeck had been employed by the owners to reside at the mine, but an eye condition forced him to seek medical attention in San Francisco. In his absence, Werninger took over the Red Cloud and declared that it was legally his because he had filed a claim and the former owner had failed to do the assessment work required by law. Though tools and equipment at the mine were valued at nearly one half million dollars, Werninger refused to allow Siebeck or the owners on the property. The matter went to court, but a judge ruled against the would-be claim jumper.

Leasers operated the Red Cloud for the next several years. Two Californians, A. G. Hubbard and George Bowers, worked it in the late Eighties and seem to have turned a profit. Their mine superintendent, Charles Pickenback, was one of the best mine operators in Arizona Territory and later helped them garner a fortune on the Clip and the Harqua Hala Bonanza. When they struck water at the five hundred foot level in 1888, Pickenback brought in a steam hoist to try to dry it up, but failed. They let their lease expire and two Yuma men, Frank Van Ness and Frank Vomocil, took it over to work the low grade ore above the water line.

Mining in the Red Cloud cost Vomocil his life. He had experienced several attacks of lead poisoning while mining at Castle Dome in earlier years. The galena in the Red Cloud brought on the malady again in 1899, and he died after fighting the disease four months.[14] He was forty-seven at the time,

[14]*Ibid.*, Nov. 4, 1882; May 30, 1885; Nov. 11, 1899.

but had been mining in Yuma County nearly twenty-three years. Taylor McCleod, another Silver District veteran, died of lead poisoning later the same year.

Red Cloud closed down after Vomocil's death and remained closed for several years. It was reopened briefly during the First World War, and again during World War II when there was a good demand for lead. In recent years gem and rock collectors have been entering the Red Cloud in search of wulfenite, a square red gem that brings high prices among the rock hound fraternity.

Clip Mine turned out to be the biggest silver producer in the district, though it was discovered later than the others. José Maria Mendivil, discoverer of the Apache lode at Picacho, located the Clip in either 1880 or 1881. He sold it to Milton Santee for $150. When Santee's exploratory drilling started showing assays of seventy ounces silver to the ton, he had no difficulty in selling it to Hubbard and Bowers for $11,500.[15] They built a stamp mill by the river, two miles above Red Cloud Gate, and cut a road through the mountains over a winding route six miles long. When production commenced in 1883, the Clip began to steadily produce between ten and fifteen thousand dollars worth of silver a month. Before they finally shut the Clip down in 1888 due to declining silver prices and low grade ore, it had returned the two California owners $750,000 in dividends.

Silver District was remote from civilization, and life must have been dull and monotonous. Gun play enlivened things from time to time, and lowered the population. One event that broke the monotony and perhaps helped the miners forget the brutal summer heat occurred in 1881 when the district's two saloon owners settled their business rivalry with firearms. Paul Billicke, a German immigrant who operated a combination saloon and restaurant, won the contest. Don MacCleod, partner in the Pacific Exchange Saloon with J. J. Stein, came out on the short end, dead from a shotgun blast.

[15]*Ibid.*, Aug. 17, 1895.

MacCleod was the aggressor. He went to Billicke's place on the morning of July 10 and became embroiled in an argument with him. When the argument became heated, MacCleod slapped Billicke in the face and rode off. He returned later in the day, pulling his pistol from its holster as he neared the German's saloon. Billicke came out with a shotgun and ordered him to leave. When MacCleod kept advancing, Billicke cut him down.

The German fled to Yuma with Taylor MacCleod, the dead man's brother, in hot pursuit. Billicke wisely turned himself over to the sheriff, and the revenge-seeking brother decided to let the law take its course. A coroner's jury decided the killer had acted in self-defense, and he was released.

When the Red Cloud closed down, Billicke gave up the saloon business and began chloriding mine dumps. Chloriders were scavengers of sorts who dug through the dumps looking for sulphurets, black granules of silver that had been missed in the milling process. Though the practice sometimes brought good returns, the mining fraternity looked on the chloriders as the lowest rung of society. Billicke fell victim to tuberculosis a decade later, and died in Los Angeles in 1892.

The old Silver District has been nearly deserted for years now. One picks up the papers from time to time to read of some weekend explorer who has fallen into one of the old mine shafts that dot the area, or perhaps of a band of hippies who have decided to call the area home. It may spring to life again some day if the price of silver ever rises high enough, or if another national emergency should create a strong demand for lead. The miners who had worked there during the Eighties always said the capitalists from the east who exploited the Silver District were incompetent. The *Sentinel* agreed, and said there were still "millions in it."[16]

[16]*Ibid.*, July 16, 1881; June 23, 1883; Jan. 31, 1885.

CHAPTER EIGHT

GOLD IN THE HARQUA HALAS

THE HISTORY of the famous Bonanza Gold Mine in the Harqua Hala Mountains of Arizona is another demonstration of how British mine investors lost fortunes when they chose to buy American mining properties. The Englishmen who bought the Bonanza lost nearly seven hundred thousand dollars while operating it. A miner once remarked that Englishmen declined the word "Miner" as: mine, miner, minus. Their record with the Bonanza is proof he was nearly right.

There was gold in the Harqua Halas, plenty of it. Americans who mined there made a great deal of money. Two operators, Hubbard and Bowers, became millionaires from their endeavors. But when Englishmen tried to get in on what appeared to be a good thing, it turned out quite differently.

It was common knowledge that the Harqua Halas contained gold for as long as twenty years before the big strike was made in 1888, but it is not clear who first discovered it. *Mining and Scientific Press* reported as early as 1869 that a Pima Indian had made a big strike in the "Harquehila Mountains,"[1] but the San Francisco *Chronicle* asserted many years later that an army officer first struck gold there, only to be driven off by Apaches. The same newspaper stated that five prospectors had managed to slip into the area while the Apaches were on the rampage and take $36,000 in surface gold before clearing out several days later.[2]

[1]*Mining and Scientific Press*, Feb. 20, 1869, p. 118.
[2]*Arizona Sentinel*, Dec. 22, 1888, quoting *San Francisco Chronicle*, n.d.

Apaches were no longer a serious menace in Western Arizona by the late 1870s, and prospectors began to comb the area with some minor successes. Socorro Mine, six miles southeast of present day Wenden, may have been the first gold mine worked extensively in the area. It was owned by a San Francisco firm, the Oro Mining and Milling Company, who began mining the Socorro in 1882. Arizona's governor, Frederich A. Tritle, and Charles Harris, a Civil War veteran, bought the mine in 1886 and built a mill four miles west, near an old water hole that had been used by Forty-niners. They named the millsite Harrisburg and began processing ore from the Socorro and a few other claims. The operation must have prospered for a time because a post office was opened at Harrisburg in 1887. Bill Bear, an old prospector known as "the Burro Man," was appointed postmaster.

Gold Mountain claim, the fabulously rich discovery that became known as the Harqua Hala Bonanza, was located by a trio of prospectors: Harry Watton, Robert Stein, and Mike Sullivan. There are two versions to the discovery story. One is that the three were dry washing in a gulch near Harrisburg on November 14, 1888 when Watton became tired and decided to climb a nearby hill. He noticed a piece of rock lying on top of a palo verde root, and kicked it out of his path. It seemed quite heavy for such a small stone, so he stooped and picked it up. It was a nugget worth $2,000. After informing his partners of his luck, the trio picked up another $25,000 worth of nuggets in three days, and found the ledge they came from.[3]

The other version is more intriguing, but less likely. John Agaard, owner of the Yum Yum Mine near Harrisburg, told it to Roscoe Willson, longtime historical writer of the *Arizona Republic*. According to Agaard, Watton and Stein had located several minor claims near Harrisburg, and Sullivan had one adjoining a claim of theirs. While Sullivan was prospecting one day, he picked up a pocket of nuggets, only to discover that

[3]H. J. Minhinnick, "Some Bonanza Mines of Yuma County," *Progressive Arizona*, II, 3 (March 1926), p. 25.

he was on the claim belonging to Watton and Stein. After convincing himself that his own claim held no such riches, he approached the two men and suggested that they combine their claims, since all were so close together. Not knowing that Sullivan had found valuable float on their claim, the pair agreed. Sullivan produced his nuggets once the deal had been made, and the trio traced the float to the Bonanza ledge.[4]

The second version is probably fictional. When the first public report of the strike was recorded in the *Sentinel* on December 8, 1888, it credited Watton with the discovery.

There was no attempt to keep the big strike a secret. Stein realized that publicity would help them sell their claim, and wrote a long letter to his friend John Dorrington, editor of the *Sentinel*, bragging about the mines. His letter was published in the December 22 issue. Stein said that ". . . the new strike has never been equalled in Arizona . . . The Gold Mountain Claim is an immense body of extremely rich ore. Boulders of float weighing from one to five tons are worth $50 to $1000 a ton. We have picked up thousands of dollars in pure gold ranging from an ounce to over $200 . . . all this laid on the surface below the ledge and in digging we found the most wonderful rich ore hanging together with gold. For the last two weeks we have taken out every day very rich ore worth hundreds per ton . . ."

Watton, Stein, and Sullivan had two claims they thought to be the richest. The Gold Mountain or Bonanza Claim was eight miles directly south of present day Salome, a town which didn't exist in 1888. The partners were also optimistic about their Golden Eagle claim, which was a mile north of the other.

The letter to the *Sentinel* set off a migration toward the Harqua Halas with several hundred prospectors hastening to the area to stake claims as near to the original ones as possible.

[4]Roscoe Willson, "Slabs of Gold As Big As a Man's Hand," *Arizona Days and Ways Magazine* of *The Arizona Republic* (Phoenix), Oct. 25, 1964, pp. 34-35.

"Miners are arriving from all directions; some as far away as Los Angeles," the *Sentinel* reported early in January.[5]

One of the first arrivals was the notorious law officer and gun fighter, Wyatt Earp. He staked out a claim five miles southeast of Gold Mountain, which he called the "Sore Finger." When it didn't provide an instant fortune, Earp sold the claim to John Rarick, who began mining it and processing the ore with an arrastra. The new owner claimed to be getting $40 a ton by that primitive method.

Harrisburg became a boom town with the hundreds of miners pouring in. By March 1890, it could boast four stores, three saloons, three restaurants, a butcher shop, blacksmith shop, post office, and several residences. Like other towns in the West which sprang into being in a few months, Harrisburg was soon having its share of shootings and fights. The first death came less than two months after the big strike. Alonso Johnson, a twenty-two year old lad from Yuma, got into a saloon argument with Peter Burns, a recent arrival from Phoenix. When Johnson picked up a wrench and threatened to use it on Burns, the other man pulled his gun and shot him dead. A coroner's jury was convened, which decided that Burns had acted in self-defense, and he was released.[6]

A young miner who came to grief at Harrisburg was John Doten. When he tangled with the newly-appointed deputy sheriff and justice of the peace, Frank Wells, in May 1890, he came out on the losing end and charged the officer with assault and battery. A Yuma jury heard the evidence against Wells and acquitted him. It seemed Doten had not learned his lesson. Two months later he got into a fight with Antonio Herrera and won by splitting his opponent's skull with an axe. He pleaded self-defense in the trial that followed, but a jury thought differently, and handed him a ten-year sentence for manslaughter.[7]

[5]*Arizona Sentinel*, Jan. 5, 1889.
[6]*Ibid.*, Jan. 19, 1889.
[7]*Ibid.*, July 12, 1890; Apr. 2, 1892.

Watton and his partners were asking $400,000 for their claims. W. S. Lyle, a mine expert sent to examine them, said the price was too high. "If anyone says there is no good ore in the district, they are wrong," Lyle reported, "but the owners of the property ask too much for their prospects to secure a purchaser from any legitimate mining company."[8]

With no buyer in sight who was willing to pay their asking price, the three partners entered into an agreement with the owner of the stamp mill at Harrisburg to process their ore. The first eight day run on Bonanza quartz produced a bar of bullion worth $2,000 as well as a ton of concentrates which were to be shipped to Colorado for further processing.

The good reports on the early production brought Douglas Gray to Harqua Hala to check out the mine in March 1889. After taking six-hundred pounds of sample ore from the two claims, Gray forwarded it to the Grand Central Mill at Tombstone for processing. Reports came back that the samples varied in value from more than $500 a ton to $231.50 a ton. Gray and his partner, Kirkland, offered $50,000 for the two claims.[9]

Watton and Sullivan were willing to accept the offer, but Stein wanted more money. Gray and Kirkland decided to buy the first two out, while Stein held his one-third share in hopes of getting more money.[10] The new owners told the press they thought they could recover their investment within ninety days.

Hubbard and Bowers, the two Californians who had operated the Clip and the Red Cloud in Silver District, were looking for a new investment. Clip had suspended operations in 1888 after paying them nearly $750,000 in profits. After a visit to the Harqua Hala District in August 1889, Hubbard decided to try to buy Stein's interest in the Bonanza and Golden Eagle. He

[8]*Ibid.*, Jan. 19, 1889.
[9]*Ibid.*, June 8, 1889.
[10]*Ibid.*, Aug. 3, 1889.

succeeded, though the price he paid was never disclosed. Stein used the money to return to Germany, the country of his origin.

Less than a year of mining convinced Hubbard and Bowers that the Bonanza Mine was all they expected it to be, and they bought out Gray and Kirkland. If a report in the *Mining and Scientific Press* on November 29, 1890, is correct, they must have paid $100,000 for the two men's claims. They reportedly gave Gray $50,000 for his. Having gained a free hand in the management, they brought in Charley Pickenback, their fore-man from the Clip, to manage the Bonanza. They also made plans to build their own mill. Until that time, the old five stamp mill at Harrisburg was processing their ore. Not only was it inefficient, but they had to share the proceeds with H. E. Harris who owned it.

The new twenty stamp mill was built near the mine and was crushing sixty tons of ore a day within a year's time. A second mining camp, Harqua Hala, began to grow up around the mines. The camp could claim a population of one hundred and fifty by July 1891, and the miners began constructing a school house the following spring.

It was generally known that Bonanza Mine was making Hubbard and Bowers rich. Arizona's Secretary of State, W. O. Murphy, bragged to the *Engineering and Mining Journal* that "an $81,000 bar of gold was turned out in a 40 day run" in 1892.[11] Even San Francisco was amazed a year later when the partners sent a three hundred and nine pound bar of gold to San Francisco, the result of a twenty-eight day run. Califor-nians said it was the largest gold brick that had ever been seen there.[12]

Gold from the Harqua Hala mines was deliberately cast into large bars to discourage theft. Robbers intent on stealing it while it was being transported to the railroad at Sentinel would find it difficult to carry away a chunk of bullion on horseback weighing one or two hundred pounds. The idea worked, and

[11]*Engineering and Mining Journal*, May 7, 1892, p. 503.
[12]*Arizona Sentinel*, Jan. 28, 1893.

bandits never tried to rob the buckboards carrying the bullion, but it did cause problems at least once.

Two deputy sheriffs, Frank Burke and George Davis, were transporting a large bar of gold to Sentinel in March 1890. When they reached the Gila River, they started across in a boat tied there for that purpose. It was their luck to have the boat capsize. Davis had enough presence of mind to grab the bar of gold as the craft started to overturn, and it carried him to the bottom of the river. Fortunately, the river was shallow, and the two law officers were able to quickly recover the lost gold.

High grading was a constant problem at the Bonanza because the ore was so rich. It became evident this would be a matter of concern for the operators from an incident that occurred at El Rio Mill west of Yuma less than two months after the mine had been located.

Two men appeared at El Rio in January 1889, and asked the superintendent for permission to crush some ore. The request immediately aroused his suspicion, and he asked them where they got it. The pair replied that it came from a mine they had discovered fifty miles from the Harqua Halas. They said they were on their way to Los Angeles to sell their mine, and needed some grub money.

The mill manager figured they had some low grade ore from a small claim and granted his permission. The two dumped eight pounds of quartz from a sack into a mortar and crushed it. After mixing the crushed ore with quicksilver, which adheres to gold, they burned off the mercury by roasting the residue on a shovel. To the surprise of mill employees, they had 7½ ounces of gold worth $135. After they left, the mill workers decided the two men were high graders from the Harqua Hala.

Mrs. Rose Johnson, who was living at the site of Harqua Hala in 1953, said that high grading was an open secret among the Mexican miners. She told a magazine writer that the miners "were ignorant fellows, peons out of Old Mexico brought in to do the heavy work for the lowest pay. But I guess they

David Neahr's store in Yuma, around 1878.

—*Courtesy Yuma County Historical Society.*

weren't so dumb," she added. "They used to be the smokingest workmen ever to mine gold, and it was a long time before the mine owners learned they were high grading the richest ore in their pipes."[13]

Arizona juries may have regarded high grading as a fringe benefit for miners if the actions of one Yuma County jury are a true indicator. Francisco Chaves and José Granillo were arrested for high grading at the Bonanza in February 1893. A Yuma jury found them "not guilty" even though they had confessed their guilt to Deputy Sheriff Frank Wells when he arrested them. So enraged at the verdict was the mine-owning editor of the *Sentinel* that he pontificated that "there seems to be an impression among a good many men that any rich specimens found in a mine belong to the finders."[14]

Bonanza Mine made the big news, but other claims in the Harqua Halas produced some gold, too. Golden Eagle Mine, which Hubbard and Bowers had purchased with the Bonanza property, produced several thousand dollars worth of gold, but was generally disappointing considering earlier assays. Barney Quinn, who owned the Golden King claim next to the Golden Eagle, reportedly took $170,000 worth of ore from his mine. Yum Yum Mine was another minor producer, but production information is scanty.

Newspaper stories about the Bonanza may have interested English promoters. *Mining and Scientific Press* told its readers that Englishmen were examining Bonanza ore in January 1891.[15] Legal difficulties are probably the reason that two years elapsed before a sale was consummated. The Alien Land Law of 1887 forbade foreigners to own more than twenty per cent of the stock of any American mining company. The penalty for violating the rule was forfeiture of the property.

Clever lawyers eventually devised a way around the restrictive law. Foreigners would set up an operating company

---

[13]Jay Ellis Ransom, "Harquahala Bonanza," *Desert Magazine*. XVI, 11 (May 1953), p. 16.

[14]*Arizona Sentinel*, Apr. 1, 1893.

[15]*Mining and Scientific Press*, June 10, 1891, p. 20.

through American citizens acting as accomplices. The operating company would purchase the mines in its own name, mine the ore, and send a major portion of its profits to the foreigners who had advanced the purchase money.

It was announced in early June 1893 that Hubbard and Bowers had sold their claims for $1,250,000. To meet the criteria established under the Alien Land Law, the purchasers were a corporation founded in St. Paul, Minnesota. Its papers of incorporation asserted that it was owned by A. Wartenweiler of St. Paul, Henry Bratnober of San Francisco, and Francis Muir of Surrey, England.

The St. Paul corporation was only a legal front for an English firm, the Harqua Hala Gold Mining Company, Limited, whose chairman was Francis Muir, one of the St. Paul incorporators. Its stock was floated on the London market in June 1893, but sales were slow. English investors had just been stung by the failure of an Arizona mine, the Seven Stars at Prescott. *Engineering and Mining Journal* commented that the stock was sold "only with a great deal of persuasion and canvassing . . . The property excites no interest at all." The price was quoted at 18 pounds a share in September.[16]

Hubbard and Bowers made a fortune on the deal. Their expenses during nearly four years of operation had been only $150,000 while they produced gold worth $1,300,000. They paid a commission of $250,000 to the brokers who sold the mines. They must have cleared at least one million dollars apiece at Harqua Hala, but as luck would have it, only one lived to enjoy the windfall. George Bowers died of Bright's disease only a few weeks after the sale was finalized. He left an estate of $4 million.[17] A. G. Hubbard was luckier. He and his wife set out the next spring to visit Europe.

The Englishmen had their own ideas about how to run a mine and began making changes soon after taking possession. Mexican miners were discharged, and replaced by miners of

[16]*Engineering and Mining Journal*, Dec. 9, 1893, p. 599; July 8, 1893, p. 40; Sept. 16, 1893, p. 310.

[17]*Arizona Sentinel*, June 24, 1893; July 8, 1893.

Anglo-Saxon origin.[18] That may have been the first mistake. The camp was soon visited by a siege of dysentery, a malady from which the Mexicans seemed to have some immunity. Francis Muir had the unpleasant duty of telling his shareholders that an inspection of the camp showed sanitary condition to be poor. He suggested the establishment of a company boarding house and the cultivation of a vegetable garden as a means of warding off future epidemics.

Hubbard's experienced foreman, Charley Pickenback, was discharged in October 1893, and replaced by an Englishman named Oxnam who had worked for the promoters at the Lamar Mine in Idaho. Pickenback stopped in Yuma to chat with the editor of the *Sentinel* on the return trip to his home in Los Angeles. He told the newspaperman that he had bet George Bowers $500 that he could turn out $180,000 worth of gold in his first six months as foreman. Pickenback won the bet by producing $196,000 worth of metal. He said A. H. Hubbard had expressed appreciation for his loyalty and skill by giving him $10,000 when the Bonanza was sold.[19]

It was soon evident that the Englishmen were having problems they had not anticipated. Ore from the first level in the Bonanza was soon nearly exhausted, and what remained was worth only $8 to $10 a ton. The quartz from the lower levels didn't seem to be much better, so company officials ordered drilling to begin on a sixth level in hopes that it would be richer.

Trouble seemed to come in batches. Rain washed away much of the company pipeline, forcing closure of the mill for several days. A second storm struck only a few weeks later, and a boiler accident shut down the mill again till repairs could be made. The superintendent complained that they had only been able to operate the mill twenty-one days in July. A worse blow came when the main shaft at the Bonanza was determined to be unsafe, and a new shaft had to be drilled. Work stopped for three months while workmen prepared the new entrance.

[18]*The Oasis* (Nogales, Arizona), Aug. 31, 1893.
[19]*Arizona Sentinel*. Oct. 14, 1893.

Not all of the problems were directly related to the technical end of mining. Stockholders began to worry about a rumor that the English investment company did not have clear title to the Arizona property. The directors published a notice in the *Engineering and Mining Journal* to reassure them that things were all right. Other stockholders complained about the need to drill a new shaft. The editors of the *Journal* expressed their feelings by commenting that "the report issued when the company was floated said nothing about a faulty shaft."[20]

Yuma's *Sentinel* stirred up trouble, too. The editor began a campaign to force the county to raise the tax assessment on the English-owned mines. He pointed out to his readers that the mines had been sold for $1,250,000, but that they were only being taxed as worth $40,000. "We only wish to ask the taxpayers of Yuma County," shrilled the *Sentinel*, "what they think of a foreign corporation being allowed to pass through the hands of the board at a paltry $40,000."[21] The Board of Equalization was properly chastised, and raised the assessment the following year.

The new shaft was completed in March 1894, but it seemed trouble had only begun. Rumors were soon flying in London investment circles that the ore was depleted in the Bonanza. Mr. Wartenweiler was dispatched to Arizona to check on the story, and forced to admit there was some truth to it. The pure quartz had played out and only porphyry with some quartz mixed in it was being found. He tried to reassure the investors by telling them that he thought it would still bring from $10 to $16 a ton. "I can see no reason why the porphyry should not be ore-bearing," he reported hopefully.[22]

While production was falling, the management tried desperately to find some way out of their plight. They tried mining ore from the Golden Eagle, a claim Hubbard and Bowers had touched only lightly. The reason soon became clear. None of it was worth more than $14 a ton, and some brought as low

[20]*Engineering and Mining Journal,* Dec. 16, 1893, p. 599.
[21]*Arizona Sentinel,* Sept. 9, 1893; Aug. 4, 1894.
[22]*Ibid.,* Apr. 4, 1894.

as $2 a ton. When the company announced in January 1895 that they were installing cyanide vats to process the tailings dumps, rumors flew that the Bonanza was finished. The London correspondent for the *Engineering and Mining Journal* added fuel to the stories by saying that the company was in a "precarious condition," and the stock dropped to an all-time low of three pounds a share.[23] Investors hoped the rumors weren't true, but feared that they were when news was released that miners were cutting down the pillars in the stopes at the Bonanza for the ore they contained. It came as an anticlimax when the directors told them in October 1895 that the ore was indeed exhausted. An attempt was made to soften the blow by informing them that the firm was considering the purchase of another gold mine in Kalgoorlie, Western Australia.

The English firm processed tailings until late in 1896. Cutting down pillars in the stopes caused a great cave-in at the Bonanza in March of that year, which created the huge cavity old-timers named the "Harqua Hala Glory Hole."[24] Leasers worked the mines for the next several years with little success. By the summer of 1899, the Englishmen decided to end their involvement by selling the mines at public auction.

It had been an expensive experience. They had produced but $694,525 in gold at a profit of $125,000. When it is taken into account that they paid $1,250,000 for the mines, the conclusion follows that their loss was in excess of a million dollars.

Anthony G. Hubbard, one of the partners who sold them the mine, had still one more surprise in store for the Englishmen. When the property was auctioned in August 1899, Hubbard offered the high bid of $5,010. It must have seemed to the owners that he was deliberately trying to add insult to injury, and they rejected his bid as being too low. Several weeks later, Hubbard met with C. H. Lindley, attorney for the English company, and it was agreed that Hubbard could have the mines at a price of $7,000.[25]

[23]*Engineering and Mining Journal*, May 4, 1895, p. 429.
[24]*Arizona Sentinel*, Mar. 21, 1896.
[25]*Yuma Sun*, Aug. 18, 25, 1899.

It would make a good ending from the American point of view if the historian were able to record that Hubbard found another million dollars worth of ore that the English operators had overlooked. But that wasn't the case. Even though the Californian brought in his old foreman, Charley Pickenback, to direct mining, the ore was gone, and Hubbard was realist enough to recognize the fact. He discharged his fifty mine and mill employees early in January 1900, and it looked as though the old Bonanza was dead forever.

But Hubbard had still not lost his magic touch. He sold the Bonanza and Golden Eagle to J. B. and Ancil Martin for $40,000 in May 1904. The Martins held the property a few years and sold it to a Michigan firm, the Ironwood Development Company, in 1906, for a rumored price of $250,000. The eastern company installed a 5,000 foot tramway connecting the Bonanza and Golden Eagle Mines, and began looking for ore bodies. By fall they announced they had discovered a vein in the Golden Eagle. The next spring, they claimed to have re-discovered a lost vein in the Bonanza.[26]

It cannot be denied that they had found some ore, because they produced $102,000 in gold in two years, but most of it probably came from the Golden Eagle rather than the Bonanza. The *Sentinel* thought that the operators were working the same vein Barney Quinn had mined in the adjoining Golden King fifteen years earlier.[27] When the ore gave out in late 1907, the mines closed down again.

Several small attempts have been made to mine on the property since that time, but without much success. Perhaps the ore is all gone, but when one considers the way humans scramble about in old mines in search of lost ledges, it wouldn't be surprising to find the Harqua Hala mines in the news again some day.

[26]*Arizona Sentinel*, May 2, Nov. 21, 1906; Apr. 10, 1907.
[27]*Ibid.*, May 15, 1907.

Chapter Nine

HEDGES — TOUGHEST MINING CAMP IN THE WEST

Mining is a dangerous occupation wherever it is conducted, but the mines in the Cargo Muchachos a few miles west of the Colorado River near Yuma may have been the most hazardous in the Southwest. Cave-ins and fires were common. Adding to the misery of the workers was the fact that wages were low, and living conditions so deplorable that the miners called one of the boarding houses "the hogpen."[1] Shootings and suicides were the normal course of events and probably reflected the unhappiness of the men who had to make their living there.

The Cargo Muchacho District was discovered in 1862 by a party of travelers bound for Los Angeles. One of their mules strayed while camped near the mountains, and they sent several boys looking for it. The animal was captured in the foothills, and one sharp-eyed lad picked up a nugget at the spot. When he showed his chunk of gold to his traveling companions, the entire party combed the area for more of the same. A few pieces of float were found, which they traced to quartz ledges in the Cargos. Subsequent investigation showed that the deposits were low grade ore, with the exception of one claim, the Cargo Muchacho.

History has forgotten the names of the 1862 travelers, and ownership of the Cargo Muchacho claim is impossible to trace until the late Seventies, when it came into the possession of Chris Horner, a Yuma blacksmith, who also owned the Padre and Madre claims in the same area. Horner sold all three to William VanArsdale and William Sublette of Oakland.

[1]*Arizona Sentinel*, Dec. 7, 1895.

E. R. Ogilby, a San Francisco mine promoter, offered the pair $30,000 for the mines in 1877, believing that he would be able to sell them for more than twice that amount to some English investors. They accepted his offer, but when Ogilby learned that they had not paid Horner in full, he sued to cancel the agreement, and a court decision returned them to Van-Arsdale and Sublette.[2] The name "Ogilby" that marks the railroad stop on the Southern Pacific near the mines serves as a constant reminder of the deal which was never consummated.

VanArsdale and Sublette decided to work the mines themselves when the deal fell through, and made an arrangement with the El Rio Mill to process their ore on a percentage basis. The plan worked satisfactorily for several years in spite of having to haul the ore ten miles to the mill.

When their contract with El Rio Mill terminated in the fall of 1881, VanArsdale leased the mill as an individual and continued milling ore belonging to the partnership. Sublette soon yelled "Foul!" in a San Francisco court, where he told the judge that his partner was pocketing all the mining proceeds and refused to give him an accounting. Until the judge could decide who was at fault, he ordered the mining operation shut down.[3]

The mines remained closed until 1889, when a Boston firm which owned the exhausted Paymaster Mine, twenty-six miles northwest of the Cargo Muchacho, purchased the claims. Lloyd Tevis and Hiram Blaisdell were principal stockholders in the Paymaster Mining Company.

The new owners decided to move the fifteen stamp mill they had been using at the Paymaster rather than have the expense of transporting ore to El Rio. A long pipeline was built to bring water from the river, and Blaisdell took over as general manager at Cargo Muchacho. He had been in charge of the firm's earlier silver mining operation at the Paymaster.

Blaisdell was an ambitious man of many interests, who was later responsible for building the first electric generating plant

[2]*Ibid.*, Mar. 15, 1879.
[3]*Ibid.*, Dec. 3, 1881.

for the city of Yuma. While he was in charge of the Cargo Muchacho Mine, he founded a Yuma newspaper, *The Times*, which provided the *Sentinel* with their first serious competition.

John Dorrington, editor of the rival *Sentinel*, must have been pleased to learn that the mining camp run by his competitor was seething with discontent, and he lost no time in publishing the information. Much of the worker dissatisfaction centered around mining methods. The management had tried to economize in timbering the Cargo Muchacho shafts by using cheap cottonwood. A serious cave-in on September 8, 1890 was the immediate result.

A three man crew, Stofella, Hernandez, and Rivas were working the night shift when the accident happened. Minor cave-ins had been common, and when Hernandez noticed that a piece of the ceiling was about to fall, he yelled to Stofella to be careful, and continued with his work. Stofella worked until two in the morning when he began wondering why he had heard nothing from the other two employees. Upon investigating, he discovered that there had been a cave-in behind them and that they were trapped. He spread the alarm and the miners were rescued unharmed after a fifty-six hour effort.

The accident at the Cargo Muchacho provided Dorrington with the ammunition he needed to flay Blaisdell. He reported that miners only worked for Blaisdell when they couldn't find work elsewhere. They were afraid of the mine because of its cottonwood timbering. Hernandez said he had complained to foreman Frank Guerra, on the night of the accident, that there was danger of a cave-in, and that the cottonwood was seldom more than five inches thick and so green that it oozed sap. Dorrington solemnly commented that "no lives were lost but the lesson taught is a serious one and cannot soon be forgotten or overlooked by those most directly concerned."[4]

Another accident at the mine the following spring seriously injured Frank Guerra, the foreman. He was climbing a ladder in the main shaft in May 1891, near the level where Hernan-

Ibid.. Sept. 13, 1890.

Hedges (Tumco) 1905.

—*Courtesy Yuma County Historical Society.*

dez and Rivas had earlier been trapped. A piece of rock dislodged and struck him on the head above the ear. Guerra was able to hold onto the ladder until he was assisted from it. If he had fallen to the bottom of the shaft, he would have probably been killed.[5]

Before the Cargo Muchacho mines closed down forever in 1895, there were several more serious accidents. Nels Munson was injured by falling rocks on December 31, 1891, and a blasting explosion seared a miner's face the next month. The victim of the accident, Murphy, was responsible for his own injury. He loaded powder into two holes and lit the fuses. When one load failed to fire, he carelessly started digging the powder out, and it exploded in his face.

While mining was beginning to peter out at the Paymaster mines, the Gold Rock mines farther north along the Cargos were just getting started. Pete Walters, a railroad section hand assigned to Ogilby Station, discovered the first vein on January 6, 1884.[6] After he filed several claims, other prospectors got wind of his strike and began locating mines.

Some of the Gold Rock claims assayed as high as $150 a ton. Walters said that he personally netted $114 on one sack of ore that he milled with an arrastra. In spite of the miners' assertions, no one was immediately eager to begin developing the veins. A fourteen mile haul would be needed to get the ore to the nearest mill at El Rio. Some of the owners thought of the possibility of sending ore by rail to San Francisco, but the Southern Pacific was demanding $40 a ton to transport it. Such rates seemed fantastic, since it cost the mine owners at Calico only a third as much to ship their ore all the way to Denver.[7]

A group of California investors decided to gamble on the Gold Rock mines in 1893 and formed the Golden Cross Mining and Milling Company. Pete Walters sold his claims for $75,000 and the firm eventually gained control of the Golden Cross, Golden Queen, General Miles, Sutton, Black Hawk, and Union

[5]*Ibid.*, May 16, 1891.
[6]*Ibid.*, Aug. 22, 1885.
[7]*Ibid.*, Jan. 3, 1885.

claims. The owners of the corporation were George S. Mullins, Thomas Fuller, E. C. Fuller, C. L. Hedges, and W. V. Hedges. They established an office at Gold Rock Camp, and began building a forty stamp mill. A town was soon flourishing around the mines, which the company named Hedges, in honor of the firm's vice-president.

The Golden Cross Mining Company had only been in operation a short time when miners began to complain of mistreatment. One of them wrote anonymously to the *Sentinel* that the firm should have named itself "the White Man's Slavery Company of California." He cited many reasons. The company paid workers three dollars a day, a low wage for that time, and furnished no accommodations. Those who wished to spend the night sleeping on bare ground on company property were assessed one dollar for the privilege. In addition every miner was charged two dollars a month for the services of the company doctor. The men thought the charge exorbitant since there was not even a shanty set aside as a hospital. Prices at the company store were far above those charged at businesses in Yuma, but the miners had to trade there because the company refused to pay anyone their wages until they quit or were fired. Most of the men were broke when they took the job, so they had to trade at the company store on credit.[8]

A meat market with company ties was also a target of miner wrath. *El Progreso*, a Spanish language newspaper published for a short time in Yuma, voiced complaints that girls who traded at the market were sometimes molested by the butchers. The company denied the charge and said the editor of *El Progreso* was trying to damage the firm's good name.[9]

Dangerous working conditions were another concern. Allen McLean, the underground foreman of the Golden Cross, was crushed to death by falling rock in September 1896. Four men were buried by falling rock at the Golden Queen in December of the same year, but were rescued. A fire put the Queen out of operation for six months the following year. Robert Temple-

[8]*Ibid.*, Dec. 7, 1895.
[9]*Yuma Sun*, Nov. 9, 1900.

ton was seriously injured in a cave-in at the Golden Cross in December 1898,[10] and William Ames and Daniel Bean were killed in an explosion in the same mine two years later.[11]

Miner response to the terrible conditions at Hedges was what would be expected. The Mexican miners formed a union, Lodge No. 8 of the Alianza Hispano-Americano, which they hoped would aid them in improving working conditions. Little is known of its efforts, but it is perhaps safe to assume that it was not very successful.

Some miners used strong drink as a balm for their difficult lives. Experience showed that discontent fueled by a plentiful supply of liquor can be an explosive mixture. The mining camp had more than the normal number of killings.

Two men died when Wilson's Saloon and Restaurant was the scene of Hedges' first gun fight in 1895. The battle began when Johnson Randolph, a prospector, entered the bar to slake his thirst. Another prospector, Mulachy, was in the establishment drinking with the two Gonzalez brothers, Juan and Tirsis, when Randolph entered.

Mulachy thought he recognized Randolph as the gun fighter who killed a friend of his in the desert for claim jumping. When he accused Randolph, he was floored with a haymaker. Seeing his drinking companion being roughly handled by the stranger, Juan Gonzalez drew his six-shooter and fired at Randolph, but missed. Randolph returned the bullet and struck Juan in the stomach with a shot that proved fatal. Tirsis, seeing his brother wounded on the floor, tried to get his gun from his holster, but was downed by another Randolph bullet that went crashing into his heart. Mulachy decided to call it quits with his two friends dead, and a coroner's jury was hastily convened, which decided that the killer had acted in self-defense.[12]

Concern for a prostitute sparked a second murder in Wilson's place early the next year. The scarlet woman had been robbed

[10]*Arizona Sentinel*, Sept. 19, Dec. 12, 1896; July 3, 1897; Dec. 3, 1898.
[11]*Yuma Sun*, Dec. 16, 1898.
[12]*Arizona Sentinel*, Dec. 21, 1895.

Hedges Mill, 1905.

—*Courtesy Yuma County Historical Society.*

of $35 while pursuing her trade in one of the Hedges houses of ill-fame. A miner named Serrano, who was fond of the harlot, believed another miner, Albert Boubion, to be the thief and told several persons of his suspicions.

Serrano was having his dinner at Wilson's when Boubion entered on March 8, 1896. According to witnesses, Boubion approached Serrano's table and said, "So I am a robber, am I?" Then he broke a pitcher, from the table, over Serrano's head and sent him tumbling to the floor.

Serrano picked himself from the floor, pulled his revolver, and shot Boubion dead before the other man could use a knife he was carrying. A coroner's inquest several days later reached a verdict of not guilty by reason of self-defense.[13]

A bartender was the victim of another Hedges saloon shooting. Constable August Jarick, the local representative of law and order, entered a drinking establishment on April 14, 1899, and found a gambling game operating. Twenty-six-year-old John Crawford, a native of Azusa, was tending bar and had been left in charge. When Jarick ordered the game of chance closed down, a heated argument ensued between him and Crawford. When the bartender broke off the conversation and started to go behind the bar, Jarick shot him dead. He claimed that Crawford was going for a gun he kept there.[14]

The wild doings at Hedges were not always as deadly serious, and reports on them must have aroused much mirth in nearby Yuma. Gracie Demente's seduction tale must have been one cause for laughter.

Fifteen-year-old Gracie was a runaway. She joined Mr. and Mrs. J. M. Clark, who were traveling in a wagon from Northern California toward Yuma. Gracie told Yuma authorities that when the wagon was about thirty miles from Hedges, Mr. Clark tried to rape her. Fleeing to save her honor, the girl said she went to the Gold Rock mines, where a kindly gentleman miner named Bill Smith had taken her under his wing and

[13]*Ibid.*, Mar. 14, 1896.
[14]*Yuma Sun*, Apr. 21, 1899; *Arizona Sentinel*, May 6, 1899.

promised that he would protect her from future seductionists. So that Smith would have full legal protection in his efforts to defend the girl's honor, he appeared with Gracie before Probate Judge Abe Frank in Yuma and asked to be be named her guardian. Irate Yumans were ready to lynch Clark when they heard the story.

Two weeks later, they heard the other side, when Clark arrived in town and was told what Gracie had related to the authorities. Bill Smith did not work at the Golden Cross mines, and had never worked there. He met Clark when he offered to guide his wagon across the desert. After the trip was underway, Clark said he became aware that the guide was attempting to seduce the fifteen-year-old girl and he ordered him to leave the wagon.

Smith left as he was asked to do, but so did Gracie. The pair ran off together, and told their tall tale to the judge so that they could travel together without being subject to legal restraints on their relationship.[15]

The *Sentinel* often recorded the antics of Cargo Muchacho miners in an amused manner. Illustrative is the following which appeared in its columns on September 7, 1895:

> Two American miners of Gold Rock came to town the first of the week. One had $175 and the other $275. They proceeded on arrival to paint the town a beautiful crimson color. They succeeded so well in this that they concluded that the gambling banks had a surplus of silver and they might as well have it as not . . . Dame fortune frowned on them and they went home broke.

Golden Cross Company's miserly ways may have been due to constant financial difficulties. Ore didn't bring the high yield they expected, and they couldn't turn a profit operating the forty stamp mill they had built. The management reasoned that a simple solution would be to add another sixty stamps.

Extra mill capacity compounded their problems. It was necessary to mine some very poor ore to keep all one hundred stamps going, and the firm went further into debt. By January 1896 they owed more than $125,000, and their creditors took

[15]*Arizona Sentinel*, Sept. 28, 1895.

over the mines. Golden Cross came out of the situation very nicely by selling the entire works to the Free Gold Mining Company in 1897. The buyers were a Salt Lake City investment group headed by Isaac Trumbo, who gave a million dollars for the property, and agreed to pay the debts owed by the Golden Cross Company.

It didn't take long for Trumbo and his fellow investors to realize they had made a bad deal. Ore from the Gold Rock mines was bringing no better than $3.10 a ton, and financial disaster was soon staring them in the face. In an effort to stave off the inevitable, the firm began cyaniding the thousands of tons of tailings that had accumulated around the mines over the years. Within two years they were insolvent, and a receiver was appointed to run the mines. One after another court appointed officials tried to make the mines pay in the years that followed, but none succeeded. By 1909 the Gold Rock mines had been deserted, and Hedges was a ghost town.

There were still some optimists who thought the Gold Rock claims could be operated at a profit, and the United Mines Company took them over in 1910 to try. Though all of the old shafts were down at least a thousand feet, they reconditioned the mill and hired a crew. The camp was rechristened Tumco, an abbreviation for the company name. Low grade ore brought the enterprise to a halt soon after it was launched.

Others were willing to invest in the Gold Rock mines in spite of the many failures. Seeley W. Mudd, one of the country's best mining engineers, bought them in 1913 and found a few new ore bodies. They weren't rich enough to sustain mining, and he gave up in September 1914. Queen Mining Company was the next to try, in 1916. They gave up in disgust within a year, and sold the mill, cyanide equipment, and pipe line for junk. A final effort was made by a firm calling itself the Sovereign Mining and Development Company between 1937 and 1941.[16]

[16]Harold and Lucille Weight, "Tumco—Two Time Ghost Camp of the Cargo Muchachos," *Calico Print*, VII, 2 (February 1951), p. 4.

Several small mining companies operated profitably while the various firms mining the Gold Rock claims were going broke. Pasadena Mine, a mile north of the Cargo Muchacho, used a crew of forty to fifty men between 1888 and 1890. It shipped ore worth $12 a ton to the mill at El Rio.

Blossom Mine, two miles from the Cargo Muchacho, employed a smaller crew. Though its discoverer is unknown, its first operators were two Southern Pacific Railroad conductors, Sippy and Moreland. They hired twenty-two miners to begin blasting ore from the Blossom in 1890, which they processed through a ten stamp mill at the site. Water was piped in from the Cargo Muchacho mines at an expense of nearly $600 a month.[17] The mine was closed for a time in 1894, but reopened again in 1895 when two Los Angeles men, Holmes and Nottman, purchased it. The ore was exhausted after they had mined the Blossom for a year.

Miners named the small camp around the mine Blossom City. Not very much is known about life there, but the few news items the camp generated suggest that it was unpleasant. Even the usually intrepid Chinese were repulsed by it. Ah Sing, the cook for the mining company, went insane as the result of his residence there. He wandered off into the desert, where he presumably perished in November 1895.[18]

American Girl Mine was the last important discovery in the Cargo Muchachos. Tom Johnson found the vein three miles southeast of Golden Cross Mine sometime in 1897, and sold shares in it to H. H. Markham, an ex-California governor, and several others. They formed the American Girl Mining Company and bought the mill Blaisdell had run at the Cargo Muchacho Mine. The vein was a rich one that produced ore worth $35 to $40 a ton.

Profits were so good that the firm added $40,000 worth of new machinery in 1902 to make the extraction process more efficient. The equipment made it possible to remove all the

[17] *Arizona Sentinel*, Feb. 7, 1891.
[18] *Ibid.*, Nov. 2, 1895.

gold except about $.80 a ton, which was lost in the tailings. By 1906 the vein had been worked out.

Life was never easy for the men who dug gold in the Cargo Muchachos. The American Girl was no exception to the pattern. The *Sentinel* noted on July 19, 1905, that Frank Fleming, one of the American Girl miners, had committed suicide. He used a rifle borrowed from the mine manager, who loaned it thinking the man was going hunting. Company officials concluded that excessive liquor and oppressive heat were probably the reason Fleming killed himself.

Deserted mine in Cargo Muchachos.

—*Frank Love Photo.*

Unidentified Colorado River prospector, 1900.

—*Courtesy Yuma County Historical Society.*

CHAPTER TEN

LOST MINES OF THE LOWER COLORADO

EVERY SECTION of the Southwest has its lost mine stories, and the area around the southern Arizona-California border is no exception. Its lore includes bonanzas lost by Frenchmen, squaws, Indian braves, and even an English lord.

While popular magazines of the Western type publish lost mine stories with an amazing degree of regularity, professional historians regard them with skepticism. Such tales are generally based upon evidence which can never be checked for authenticity. The usual lost mine story came from an ancient prospector, who heard it from another prospector, whose uncle told it to him when he was a boy. Such a tenuous route is often the trail followed by much of the romance of the Old West, but it is hardly the type of material upon which a competent historian will stake his reputation.

Lost mine tales from the Lower Colorado region fit the pattern. Nearly all of them were first published in printed form during the 1890s and supposedly describe a vein or placer digging that was lost twenty or thirty years earlier.

If frequency of retelling is a barometer of truth, the Lost Frenchmen Mine may really exist. It had its origins in local literature, but has been retold often by the treasure magazines. The *Arizona Sentinel* first recorded the tale in print in a long feature article on August 6, 1892. Though the editor didn't tell where he got most of his information, he did say that he learned about the mine from Bill Bear, the postmaster at Harrisburg, a town near the Harqua Hala Mine.

Sometime in the early 1860s, the story goes, three Frenchmen came to Yuma and deposited nearly eight thousand dollars in gold at George Hooper's mercantile establishment. Hooper's firm acted as a kind of bank for local residents. After purchasing a quantity of supplies, the trio left town, heading in the direction of Aqua Caliente. They were followed by five local residents, whose curiosity had been aroused, and who surmised that the Frenchmen had discovered a new mine. If that were true, they hoped to stake claims in the same area.

The Frenchmen outdistanced their pursuers, but the five came upon them at Aqua Caliente, where they had camped for the night. There was nothing the Yumans could do but make camp nearby and wait for dawn.

Morning arrived. To the dismay of the five men who had trailed the Frenchmen, they were gone. Aware that they had been followed, the trio left in the middle of the night. To further confuse their pursuers, each of them had taken a different trail. Not knowing which trail to follow, the five local men returned to Yuma cursing their luck.

Though the Frenchmen were never again seen in Yuma, George Norton said their burros came in to Antelope Station without them. Norton, a prospector, said that Apaches were active at the time and probably killed them. He thought he found their remains in 1895 when he found some human bones thirty miles north of Mohawk Pass on the Southern Pacific. An old Apache was located, the *Sentinel* said, who remembered when they were killed.[1]

Bill Bear gave further credence to the Lost Frenchmen story. He said that he had been working as a prospector and mule driver in addition to his duties as postmaster at Harrisburg in 1899 when he was hired by a Mexican to haul water and supplies into the Eagle Tail Mountains southeast of Harrisburg. While engaged in that task, Bear said the man told him that he had once seen the Lost Frenchmen Mine and that he was searching for it.

[1]*Arizona Sentinel*, Apr. 13, 1895.

While still a boy, the Mexican said he ran away from home. He managed to survive by hiring himself out to cook for three men, who said they were going prospecting. The trio, whom he believed to be the legendary Frenchmen, took him to a camp in the mountains where there was a running spring, mesquite trees, and some cottonwoods. The boy was left in camp each day while the men disappeared. Each evening they returned, laden with nuggets.

The Mexican told Bear that his curiosity got the best of him one day, and he followed the men. He did not have far to go because they were mining less than a mile from camp. Unfortunately his presence was discovered, and his employers began mistreating him to show their displeasure. Their cruelty finally became so severe that he deserted their camp. He recalled that he had to travel several days before he was able to reach Aqua Caliente.

George Norton, the miner who found bones he thought were those of the Frenchmen, spent many years searching for the lost bonanza. He reported that he had found it in the Eagle Tail Mountains in 1895, when he located a vein of gold he dubbed the Oregonian. Norton thought it was the same vein that the French miners had been working, but after he followed it down more than a hundred feet, he decided it was worthless.[2]

Norton maintained his interest and belief in the Lost Frenchmen Mine for at least another decade. In a letter to the editor, published in the *Sentinel* on September 12, 1906, he related how Dr. DeCorse, the local physician, had once shown him some of the nuggets that he said the Frenchmen brought to Yuma. He affirmed that his faith in the mine's existence was strengthened by the discovery of an old mining camp in a cave near Squaw Peak. It contained yellowed letters written in French.

There have been many reports from time to time that someone has located the Lost Frenchmen Mine, but they have al-

[2]*Ibid.*, Aug. 6, 1892; Aug. 22, 1896.

ways proven to be false. A tale circulated in 1895 that the mine had been discovered twenty-five miles north of Aztec. The *Sentinel* said the report was false in its February 2 issue. The digging was one that had been worked several years earlier by Ramon Garcia and E. B. Waggy, the newspaper said. It was worthless and had been abandoned.

The *Sentinel* was hopeful that it might lay the tale to rest permanently. "The Frenchmen . . . never had any real existence in the opinion of our most substantial citizens," the newspaper said, "and the sooner 'amateur' miners give up the idea that it does, except in the fertile and imaginative brain of a few notorious liars and yarn spinners, the Colorado Desert will not be the scene of so many tragic deaths annually of thirst . . . Nearly all who have perished belong to the tenderfoot class of miners."

One of the "notorious liars" may have been the Harrisburg assayer, John McCasey. Not only was he a source for the Lost Frenchmen tale, but also for a yarn about a lost mine that featured an English aristocrat. "Lord" Darrel Duppa, an early settler of the Salt River Valley, was the hero of the tale. Historians generally credit Duppa with giving Phoenix its name.

McCasey said that Duppa was traveling through Penehatchapee Pass, two miles east of Harrisburg, with several companions in 1864 when he discovered a large quantity of gold quartz scattered on the ground. When the party began sacking the ore, they were attacked by Indians. The raiders were repulsed, and the travelers were able to collect eight bags of the quartz, which they carried to San Francisco. It brought between $75 and $600 a bag. Duppa returned to the pass several months later, McCasey said, but the ore they had been unable to carry off earlier was all gone.[3]

There is a faint possibility the tale may be true. Gold was reported in the Harqua Halas long before the Bonanza Mine was discovered. Some early day miner may have been mining a vein and been surprised by Indians while transporting his ore

[3]*Ibid.,* Aug. 6, 1892.

to an arrastra. He may have been killed, and the Indians might have taken his wagon and mules. Not knowing the value of the ore, they may have dumped it in the pass. Another traveler using the same pass after Duppa could have picked up the remaining quartz.

Another persistent lost mine story centers around an Indian squaw, but it has three contradictory versions. The oldest may be the one reported in the Yuma *Sun* by editor Mulford Winsor on October 1, 1897.

The Lost Squaw Mine was discovered in Spanish times, Winsor said. The conquerors of Mexico found the mine in the Adonde (now Copper Mountain) Range near Baker's Tank, and took out several million dollars in gold. For some reason known only to them, they abandoned the mine after some years.

Indians knew where the mine was located, but kept it a secret. One generation after another described its location to their young men, with the admonition that to disclose its site to an outsider meant death. Squaws were never told the location of the mine, according to Winsor, because they talk too much. One young Indian woman did learn about the mine in spite of the effort to keep the information from females.

As fate would have it, the girl who knew where the mine was located fell in love with an Englishman, Reginald Grey, who wandered into Arizona in 1851 after the gold rush in California. The lovers ran off together, but soon ran out of money.

An urgent need for cash led Grey's squaw to tell him about the old Spanish mine. When asked its location, she refused to tell him, and said her people would kill her if she told where it was. The girl said that she would go to the mine and get some ore for Grey if he promised not to follow her.

The lovers went out toward the Adondes and camped near Baker's Tank. Each day the Indian girl would go to the mine and return with a bag of ore. Grey mortared out the gold and sold it. They followed the same procedure for several months, until the girl failed to return to camp one evening. Grey searched for her several weeks, but never saw her again. He gave up after deciding that her people had learned she was taking ore from the mine and killed her.

The second version of the story is quite different and even places the mine in another area, the Harqua Halas. It comes from a source that was quite reputable, the *Arizona Mining Journal*.[4]

Two Quechan men were traveling in the Harqua Hala region with a squaw, according to the story. They picked up some rich float and sold it. Both died shortly afterward without having told anyone where they got the ore. Only the woman knew the location of the place.

Two prospectors heard about the Indians bringing the gold to Yuma and hired the squaw to take them to where it had been found. She showed them the place, but that didn't satisfy them. They demanded that she show them the vein from which the ore had come. When she replied that she had never seen the ledge, they beat her severely. During the night, she fled from the prospector's camp and vowed she would never show another person where the float had been found.

Ed Schlieffen, the celebrated discoverer of the Tombstone mines, is said to have heard the tale some years later and located the Indian woman. She would not take him to the place, but did describe it for him. He went looking for the mine, but was never able to find it. When Stein, Watton, and Sullivan made the Harqua Hala bonanza strike in 1888, Schlieffen is supposed to have remarked that the mine was in an area that perfectly matched the place the squaw described.

A third version also places the mine in the Harqua Halas, but locates it in an area somewhere south of Cullen's Well. Though the *Prescott Courier* was the original source of the tale, the *Sentinel* repeated it for the benefit of local lost mine enthusiasts on March 22, 1905.

It goes this way. Back in the days when General Crook was chastising the warring Apaches, a sick squaw appealed to

[4]John L. Riggs, "Old Traditions of the Lost Mines of the West," *Arizona Mining Journal*, VII, 4 (July 15, 1923), p. 33.

Charles Cullens, one of his officers, to allow her to remain in the area rather than be removed to a reservation. Cullens relayed the request to his superiors and it was granted.

While talking to the old squaw, Cullens noticed that she had ear rings of gold. He asked where she got them and she replied that the gold came from a mine far to the west in the desert. When the army officer asked if she would take him to the mine, she agreed to take him part of the way because of his kindness. After the woman took him some distance and gave him directions, Cullens went on alone. Before he was able to find the mine, his water ran out and he had to give up the search. Cullens died a short time later without having found the mine.

There have been several reports that prospectors have located the Lost Squaw Mine, but all have proven false. Two miners, McCarroll and Snyder, said they had found it in 1897. They discovered an old digging in the Adondes from which they claimed two or three hundred tons of ore had been removed "by the original discoverers, hundreds of years ago."[5] They filed claims on the St. Louis, Gold Bond, and Copper Mountain Mines, which were all at the southeastern end of the range. It turned out that their mines contained more copper than gold, but they insisted upon calling their claims the "Lost Squaw Group."[6] A considerable amount of copper was taken from the Copper Mountains in the next decade, but it seems unlikely that the mines were the Lost Squaw.

The Castle Dome Range is supposed to be the location of the Lost Box Canyon Mine. The *Sentinel* reported on February 13, 1892, that some Quechans hunting mountain sheep discovered the mine. The Indians wandered into a box canyon that had white and pink walls several hundred feet high. There they ran out of water. One of the party found a pool of water at the head of the canyon formed by a spring that rose from beneath the face of the canyon wall. While drinking from the

[5]*Yuma Sun*, Oct. 29, 1897.
[6]*Ibid.*, Mar. 18, 1898.

—⋖{ 131 }⋗—

pool, one of the Quechans saw that the bottom of it was covered with gold nuggets. Realizing that they would be able to trade the gold to Mexicans for mescal, knives, beads, and tobacco, they gathered up as many of them as they could find and prepared to leave. Their departure was suddenly interrupted by a flash flood which swept through the canyon. All of the Indians but one was drowned.

The surviving Quechan returned to his village on the Colorado and told the story to his tribal leader. The chief cautioned the brave to never return to the box canyon again. "The Great Spirit told us never to enter that canyon," he said. "He found it necessary to teach us a lesson."

Nick Gunther, "Long John" Bourland, and Neil Johnson told the *Sentinel* they had heard the story years earlier, and had searched for the mine. They were never able to find the canyon, and no significant amounts of gold have ever been mined from the Castle Dome Range.

The California side of the Lower Colorado has contributed the Lost Cabin Mine legend. William P. Carter, who was a guest at the Ford Hotel in Phoenix, volunteered information on the lost lode to the *Arizona Republican* newspaper in 1899, and the *Sentinel* picked up the story.[7]

Carter said that a party of prospectors discovered the vein years earlier, after they had outfitted in Yuma. The group went west into the desert, where they were attacked by Indians. Leaving the route they had planned to follow, they fled into the mountains to escape their attackers. One of the prospectors went out to find firewood the next morning, and happened upon a quartz ledge which contained "fabulous wealth."

The prospectors worked the vein until they ran short of supplies. After packing their gold on two burros, they headed back toward Yuma to replenish their larders.

When they had traveled two days, they were set upon again by Indians. Several charges were fended off, but they began to fear they would never escape carrying so much gold. Accord-

[7]*Arizona Sentinel*, Mar. 18, 1899.

ing to Carter, they buried their treasure in the crevice of a dwarfed tree.

The next Indian attack killed all but one of the prospectors. He managed to escape under cover of darkness, without food or water, but with a pocket of gold dust. After wandering in the desert for several days, he became delirious, but eventually staggered into Yuma in a state of shock. He was out of his mind for several months. When his sanity returned, everyone wanted to know where he had gotten the pocket of gold dust. He was unable to say exactly where the mine was located. He could describe the site, its landmarks, and the cabin the prospectors had built, but didn't know for certain where it was.

Carter told the newspaper that he had recently met an old miner who thought he had located the Lost Cabin Mine. It had caved-in tunnels and a fortified mouth.

Many old mines in the California mountains might fit that description, but the *Sentinel* seemed to have faith in the story. The editor commented that Indians had often wandered into Yuma in the past with gold dust. He thought it possible that they found the dust buried under the dwarfed tree.

The Lower Colorado can also boast that it has a lost placer mine that sent a group of men on a wild goose chase some years ago. According to the tale, it was first discovered along the Colorado by a group of sixteen prospectors in 1860. The gold was in a gulch near the river and extremely plentiful. Each pan of dirt contained at least one nugget, and the sixteen miners were able to gather $220,000 in gold before their supplies ran out.

Ten of the men set out for Fort Yuma to get more supplies, but they were set upon by Apaches along the trail and massacred. The Indians made off with their gold and horses. An army officer commanding a cavalry patrol from Fort Yuma, Lieutenant Bliss, is supposed to have found the bodies of the dead miners.

The story continues that the six who remained at the digging continued mining and panned out another $100,000 in gold.

The Apaches, who had killed their companions, located them and attacked their camp. Four of the miners were killed, but two of them, Keller and Wood, managed to sneak away. The army's Lieutenant Bliss found them wandering in the desert and brought them to safety at Fort Yuma.

Keller died shortly afterward, the story says. Wood returned to the Lower Colorado in 1885, to try to find the placer diggings, but failed. He blamed his lack of success on the fact that the government trail he followed was not the same as the one they had used years earlier.

Wood made a map of the area where he thought the mine was located, and either sold it or gave it to a group of greenhorns in 1905. They formed the "Belding Prospecting Syndicate" and announced to the world that they were going to find the Lost Placer Mine. There is no record that they were successful.[8]

Like many lost mine tales, the Lost Placer yarn was an outright fabrication. No Lieutenant Bliss was stationed at Fort Yuma in 1860, if the *Post Returns* kept by the commanding officer may be considered accurate. Heitman's *Historical Register . . .* even states that there was no one named Lieutenant Bliss in the entire United States Army in 1860.[9] It would seem that Wood, the man who drew the map, concocted the story to mislead the Belding people.

Maybe there is some truth to the old saw that a Western mine is no more than a "hole in the ground with a liar at the top."

[8]*Ibid.*, Mar. 15, 1905.

[9]Francis B. Heitman, *Historical Register and Dictionary of the United States Army*, Vol. I (Washington: Government Printing Office, 1903), pp. 224-225.

Chapter Eleven

THE TREASURE ALONG EL CAMINO DIABLO

AN OLD TRAIL that runs northeast from Sonora toward Yuma was the earliest route used by the Spanish padres who brought Christianity to the Indians of the Lower Colorado. It is a hot, dry, dusty route, and scores who followed it perished of thirst and heat. That the Spaniards named it the Devil's Highway is no great surprise.

As El Camino Diablo wends its way toward the river, it passes within several hundred feet of an old mine at the Southeastern end of the Gila Range. La Fortuna, as it was named, yielded three million dollars in gold around the turn of the century. What is amazing is that none of the thousands who passed that way during the California gold rush bothered to prospect in the Gilas. If they had, they might have found the Fortuna almost a half century before it was located in 1894.

Those early day Forty-niners can be excused for their oversight. The lure of California was too strong. But the Anglo prospectors who combed Southwestern Arizona after the Civil War can't use that excuse. Geologists misled them into ignoring the Gilas. They were told that the rock strata was of a type that precluded any mineral vein from going very deep into the earth.[1]

There is much confusion about the discovery of Fortuna Mine. One historian, James Barney, reported in a 1949 issue of *The Sheriff* (April) that it was discovered by three ranchers, Charles Thomas, Laurent Albert, and William Halbert. He said

[1]*Arizona Sentinel*, Mar. 28, 1896.

the men were hunting stock that had strayed from their ranches. On the evening of December 22, 1894, they camped at the southeastern end of the Gilas and built a hot fire to keep warm.

The following morning the men noticed that the fire had "melted some kind of metal with which the rocks were impregnated." After examining it, they decided that the metal was gold which had been freed from the rock by the heat of their fire. It was a simple matter to trace the float up an arroyo to a quartz vein.

Another Fortuna discovery story which was printed in the highly reputable *Engineering and Mining Journal* in 1912 gave credit to only two men, Billy Holbert (not Halbert) and an unnamed partner. The author, who the mining magazine listed as a "Special Correspondent," was not given a by-line. He said that the pair were prospectors on their way to the California placer fields in 1892 whose burros strayed. Holbert was following one of the burros and picked up a piece of rock to throw at the animal. The mining magazine's reporter alleged that Holbert was "on the point of throwing it at the leader when his trained eye caught the glint of gold. Investigation showed that the ground was literally spotted with gold-bearing rock."[2]

Nonsense! *Engineering and Mining Journal* should have checked the credentials of its correspondent more carefully. His date was two years too early, and he was two prospectors short. Barney had less excuse for his errors. He was a one-time resident of Yuma and could have found the truth by reading old copies of the *Sentinel.*

Four prospectors, not two or three, were in on the Fortuna strike. They were Peter Farrell, Laurence Albert, William "Billy" Halbert, and Charles W. Thomas. The quartet were down-on-their-luck prospectors who were so broke they had to get a grubstake on credit from a Yuma merchant.[3] It is likely

[2]"History of a Once Famous Arizona Gold Mine." *Engineering and Mining Journal*, Feb. 17, 1912, p. 372.
[3]*Arizona Sentinel*. Mar. 28, 1896.

that the date mentioned in the *Sentinel*, December 22, 1894, was the day they camped on the slopes of the Gilas near Fortuna because they named one of their nine claims the "Christmas Gift." Contemporary newspapers did not tell how they happened to find the Fortuna Lode, but the tale about throwing a rock at a burro reads too much like Henry Wickenburg's discovery of the Vulture.

The finders were frustrated in their first attempts to sell the Fortuna. Geologists said the vein couldn't go very deep due to the rock structure of the Gilas, and prospective buyers were afraid to gamble on it even with assays running as high as $300 a ton. The four were on the verge of letting it go for a pittance when County Recorder M. L. Pool decided to take a look at it. He got lost trying to find it and walked seventeen miles out of his way in the July heat. In spite of his near disaster, one look convinced him the Fortuna was all the boys said it was. Pool offered to help them sell it.

The Recorder's first step was to write to his friend Robert Strauss, a mining engineer who was working in Mexico. Strauss answered that the four should resist selling it cheaply until he had a chance to examine it. Within a month, he had been to the Fortuna and advised Charles Lane of Angel's Camp, California, that the mine would be a good buy at the $150,000 asking price.

Lane was the senior partner of Lane, Hayward, and Hobart, one of the largest mining companies on the Pacific Coast. He had helped organize the Wild Goose Company that profited from the Alaska gold rush and was operating the Utica Mine at Angel's Camp, California, in 1895.[4] Caution had been one of the secrets of his success, and he would only agree to bond the Fortuna until February 1896, with the understanding that if it didn't prove valuable, he was not liable for the $150,000 asking price.

Early reports were encouraging. The mine was down one hundred and fifty feet by October 1895, and the ore was aver-

4"History of a Once Famous . . .", *op. cit.*, p. 372.

Ore wagon at Fortuna, 1900. Reputed to be the largest in Arizona.

—*Courtesy Yuma County Historical Society.*

aging $50 a ton. It seemed certain that Lane would take up the bond on its expiration date. Johnny Speese began running a four horse stage from Blaisdell Station, twelve miles away on the Southern Pacific Railroad, to the mining camp. Three saloons were installed, with colorful names: the Bucket of Blood, the Utica, and the Blazing Star.[5]

Lane knew a good thing when he saw it! Farrell, Halbert, Thomas, and Albert received their $150,000 in February 1896. They gave $3,000 to County Recorder Pool for his help in selling their claims. Halbert and Pool promptly reinvested part of their money in Yuma's first ice house, which they constructed at Second and Main Street, and was capable of producing ten tons of ice a day. But Billy Halbert's good fortune was short-lived. He was dead in little more than two years.[6]

Charles Thomas bought a ranch in California with his share of the money, but he didn't fare much better. He was dead within six years after sale of the mine. Farrell and Albert disappeared from Yuma, and their progress afterwards is unknown.

Lane put in a twenty stamp mill, which promptly began to prove that his judgment had been good. Fortuna produced more than two million dollars worth of gold and silver in the next five years. Though the mill was able to save seventy-five per cent of the gold from the quartz, Lane was not satisfied with the milling process and added cyanide vats in 1899 to improve the extraction of the ore. The tanks removed another $5 a ton from the tailings.

The town of Fortuna was never as large as Hedges because Lane's labor force seldom exceeded one hundred, but it was a lively place for its size. It had a house of prostitution that the miners jokingly renamed "the Y.M.C.A.,"[7] and a hotel or boarding house presided over by a Chinese immigrant, Charlie

[5]*Arizona Sentinel,* Nov. 9, 1895; Jan. 11, 25, Mar. 28, 1896.
[6]*Ibid.,* Mar. 20, 1897.
[7]Information on the back of an old photograph from the files of the Yuma County Historical Society.

Fortuna Mill, 1900.

—Courtesy Yuma County Historical Society.

Sam. The University of Arizona's mineralologist, William Blake, visited Sam's establishment in 1898 and reported that the meals were good and that he kept a supply of ice water, a luxury in early day mining camps.

Payday at Fortuna usually brought an influx of visiting prostitutes and gamblers from Yuma who were intent upon parting the miners from their wages. Lane attempted to foil the denizens of the underworld in 1897 by changing payday without informing them. The *Sentinel* was amused by his efforts and commented on them. "The pay day at Fortuna Camp was changed from the 10th to the 6th this month . . . As a result our 'soiled doves' and gamblers got left a few hours, but the train of the 10th carried them all out, and though a little late we have no doubt they made up for lost time on arrival."[8]

Saloons played a role in most of the Fortuna killings. One shooting threatened to create a major incident.

It began on October 22, 1897, when Juan Juaves, an ex-convict who had been drinking in one of the Fortuna bars, was called to the doorway by José Rodriguez. As Juaves stepped outside to talk to him, Rodriguez pulled his gun and opened fire. Juaves fell dead from bullet wounds after the second shot. The killer lit out for the desert, but a posse was on his trail by morning.[9]

Rodriguez shook the posse near Yuma the next day. Two days later, Undersheriff Wilder heard that he was at a railroad construction camp at Mammoth Tanks, forty miles west of Yuma. The law officer went to the camp unaware that more than two hundred Mexican railroad employees were on strike. The strikers assumed that he was there to try to disrupt their protest action. Wilder didn't speak Spanish and was unable to tell them he was trailing a murderer. The strikers, misunderstanding his intentions, became very hostile and threatening.

The superintendent of the railroad construction crew had in the meantime telegraphed the Sheriff's Office for assistance and protection. He complained that his life had been threatened

[8]*Arizona Sentinel*, Jan. 9, 1897.
[9]*Ibid.*, Oct. 23, 1897.

Crew at Fortuna Mine, 1900.

—*Courtesy Yuma County Historical Society.*

and that some of the Anglo employees were in danger. Shortly after Wilder's confrontation with the strikers had ended, Sheriff Greenleaf arrived on the scene.

Seeing more law officers arriving, the strikers again became surly. They began throwing rocks. Wilder tried foolishly to scare them away by firing his pistol in the air. The act infuriated the strikers, and a large rock hit him in the head, forcing him to drop his gun. A striker retrieved the weapon and fired several shots in the direction of the officers. A cool-headed deputy finally put an end to the riot by advancing on them with a shotgun.

Sheriff Greenleaf used the lull to telegraph for reinforcements. When they arrived, he arrested as many strikers as he could lay hands upon and had them loaded upon railroad cars and shipped to San Diego. To his amazement, when the deportees reached California, it was discovered that the Fortuna killer, José Rodriguez, was among them. He was charged with murder and convicted.[10]

Pete Burke, the law officer who was killed in a riot at Picacho a few years later, won his spurs in a Fortuna saloon killing. One of the saloon owners hired him to run his establishment while he was gone on Sunday, May 21, 1899. He instructed Pete to collect a few overdue bills if the patrons who owed them should enter.

Guadalupe Rosales, a miner known locally as "the Bull Fighter," went into the bar while Burke was in charge. Rosales already had earned a bad reputation around the mining camps as the result of a killing at Hedges the winter before. He stabbed another miner, Solomon Gonzales, to death after being refused the loan of a dollar. When a posse set out to arrest Rosales for the murder, they accidentally killed John Lee, a black miner from Hedges, who was also trying to apprehend Rosales. The "Bull Fighter" had been captured, but was out on bond of $2500 when he went into the Fortuna bar.[11]

[10]*Ibid.*, Oct. 30, 1897.
[11]*Ibid.*, May 27, 1899.

Crew preparing to enter Fortuna Mine, 1900.

—Courtesy Yuma County Historical Society.

Rosales owed one of the bills that Burke was supposed to collect. When Burke presented it to Rosales, he not only refused to pay it, but made a move that Burke interpreted as an attempt to draw his gun. Without hesitation, Burke drew a gun he had ready behind the bar and shot Rosales.

Yuma applauded the killing. "Everybody is of the opinion," the *Sentinel* remarked on May 25, 1899, "that Mr. Burke did a good thing in ridding the county of such a dangerous element." No one was very surprised when Judge Street "ignored" the charges against Burke at the fall session of the District Court.

Fortuna was not as rough as some of the other camps because of Lane's efforts to encourage the miners to use their leisure time constructively. A baseball team was organized. Young ladies from Yuma were invited to dances at the camp, with company teams provided to transport them from Blaisdell Station to the mining town. A school was started for children of the employees. Lane provided a competent physician, Dr. H. C. Stinchfield, to minister to the medical needs of the miners. His wife, Lottie Mae, assisted him as a nurse in the two-room hospital they operated for the company.

The ore vein was suddenly lost on a fault line in 1900, and there was a frantic scramble to try to find it again. During the early years of mining, miners had followed an inclined shaft to about 350 feet. A vertical shaft was dug in an effort to find the vein, and it luckily struck a portion of it. But the vein was lost again in 1901.[12]

Lane had a practical attitude toward mining. Sentiment about an old mine's production records in the past played no part in his decision-making. "When she doesn't pay, shut her down," he told his superintendents. He made one more effort to locate the vein, and when that failed, he ordered the miners to begin shooting out the pillars of ore that had been left earlier to support the tunnels and drifts. One result was a great cave-in at the 200 foot level in 1903, but no one was hurt. Mining stopped at Fortuna in 1904.

[12]*Ibid.*, Feb. 6, 1901.

Cyanide vats at Fortuna, 1900.

—*Courtesy Yuma County Historical Society.*

There are always a few romantic souls who think they can revive an old mine after it is dead, and Fortuna was no different than the rest. A firm calling itself the Fortuna Mine Corporation tried to find the faulted vein in 1913, but failed. Another group of adventurers, the Elan Mining Company, gave it a try with the same results in 1926.[13]

Old Fortuna Mine is now on the gunnery range used by Marine pilots and is not readily accessible to visitors. Those who wish to see what remains should get permission from the Provost Marshal's Office at the Marine Corps Air Station in Yuma. Failure to do so might result in being subjected to strafing or bombing by Marine planes.

El Camino Diablo still passes within a short distance of Fortuna, but it is sandy and almost impassable in places. Trail bikes or four wheel drive vehicles are recommended for the trip.

[13]Eldred Wilson, *Geology and Mineral Deposits of Southern Yuma County, Arizona* (Tucson: University of Arizona Press, 1933), pp. 188-199.

Tyson Stage Station was center for Quartzsite mining activity.

—*Frank Love Photo.*

CHAPTER TWELVE

TWO COPPER CAMPS

COPPER did not play a major role in the mining industry of the Lower Colorado, but the metal has been found and mined in a number of places. Several small copper mines operated in the Quartzsite area around the turn of the century and also in the Copper Mountain region southeast of Yuma.

Planet and Swansea were the two most important copper camps, but their production nowhere matched that of the old mines at Jerome or the modern day producers around Globe, Miami, Superior, Douglas, or Ajo. Yet their story is a part of the Lower Colorado mining saga, and deserves to be told.

Planet Mine is nineteen miles northeast of Parker, Arizona, and less than a mile south of the Bill Williams River which forms the northern boundary that separates Yuma County from Mohave County in Arizona. It was discovered in 1863 by Robert Ryland of San Francisco, which makes it one of the oldest copper mines in Arizona.[1] Within a year, San Francisco capitalists had organized the Planet Copper Mining Company and begun working the mine with Ryland as their superintendent.

Ore from the Planet began arriving in San Francisco by Fall, 1864, and brought an incredible $100 a ton. It came from a lode that was six hundred feet long and six feet wide. Some of the ore body was forty per cent copper.

The Williams Fork District, as the area was named, grew rapidly once the Civil War was ended. Copper was bringing

[1]Nell Murbarger, *Ghosts of the Adobe Walls* (Los Angeles: Westernlore Press, 1964), p. 257.

$68 a ton for thirty per cent ore.[2] When the price of transporting the ore to San Francisco dropped to $28 a ton, the boom was on. Other mines were located that claimed ore as rich or richer than the rock from the Planet. Great Central Mine bragged that some of their ore was seventy-four per cent copper, and that they had produced a hundred tons that averaged thirty per cent in only three days.[3] Mineral Hill, Eliza, Adelphi and Empire Mine all made similar claims.

Transportation was a major problem. River steamers were available to transport ore from Aubrey Landing, two miles northeast of present day Parker Dam, but the miners could not count on them arriving regularly. There were frequent complaints that ore was piling up at Aubrey Landing. Most of the mines tried to solve the problem by building their own smelters and shipping bullion. Planet Mine continued to send its ore away for smelting, but began sending it to Swansea, Wales, where they got better results than they did from the San Francisco smelters.

The labor force was mostly Mexican and Chinese in the early days.[4] Planet Mine used American miners, but complained that the costs of labor were too high. A few Indians were employed in the mines, but there was much distrust of them. The miners blamed them for stealing the horses that were constantly disappearing. "I intend to work all summer if the Indians don't steal my teams and animals," one man wrote to the Prescott *Miner*.[5]

Copper prices fell drastically in 1867. Planet cut its work force to less than fifteen men who were instructed to remove no ore from the mine that wouldn't bring at least $80 a ton. The other mines followed their example, hoping to dig enough high grade ore to meet operating expenses. They believed

[2]*Mining and Scientific Press*, Nov. 19, 1864, p. 327; May 6, 1865, p. 275; Aug. 11, 1886, p. 86.

[3]*Ibid.*, Apr. 20, 1867, p. 246.

[4]R. G. Raymer, "Early Copper Mining in Arizona," *Pacific Historical Review*, IV, 2 (1935), p. 127.

[5]*Mining and Scientific Press*, May 16, 1868, p. 320, quoting *Miner*, n.d.

prices would soon rise again and the lower grade ore might be mined at a profit when the time came.

But prices didn't rise. Mines began to close completely in the early months of 1868, and the miners left disgruntled. Superintendent Flower of Springfield Company's Punta Del Cobre Mine returned to San Francisco saying that he wouldn't "go up or down the creek (Bill Williams River) for all the mines on it."[6] By the end of the year, all the mines were closed and the district reverted to wilderness.

Planet was quiet for the next fifteen years. Construction of the Atlantic and Pacific Railroad (now the A. T. & S. F.) across Arizona revived it for a time in 1884. Realizing that Planet Mine would be only twenty-nine miles from Bouse on the railroad line, the Matilda Mining Company took over and began digging ore. Floods hampered them in the Spring. They ran their ore through a smelter at Planet and shipped only bullion, but their Fall operations also failed to show a profit. Low copper prices, combined with high transportation costs in getting the bullion to the railroad at Bouse, proved too great a handicap. Even though they had discovered some gold in one of their mines, the firm was out of business by the end of the year.[7]

Oliver Augdahl, a local miner and entrepreneur, acquired the Planet in 1900, and began trying to sell it to outside interests. He succeeded in the Fall of 1901 when J. Stanley Jones of Colorado Springs agreed to buy it for $100,000. Jones formed the Copper Mining Company with himself as its president and put a crew to work trying to locate some new ore bodies. There were reports from time to time that they had found one, but none proved true until 1908, six years after exploration had begun. N. H. Partridge, general manager for the mine, told newspapers the miners had located a new ore body at the four hundred foot level of the mine which contained gold and copper. The miners began sinking a new shaft, and Partridge

[6]*Ibid.*
[7]*Arizona Sentinel*, July 24, 1884; Oct. 18, 1884.

was enthusiastic about its possibilities. "The Planet Mine has the reputation of being the first copper mine ever operated at a profit for any considerable length of time in the territory," he said.[8]

[8]*Arizona Sentinel*, Jan. 22, 1908.

Partridge was mistaken. The Ajo copper mines predated the Planet by at least nine years. It turned out that even his enthusiasm about the new ore body was premature. The ore was not as valuable as he thought and the firm ceased mining operations at Planet a few months later. The last recorded mining at Planet was conducted by the Northwest Leasing and Development Company which wisely confined its efforts to cutting down the old pillars in 1917. They employed forty-eight men and were able to ship 1200 tons of ore a month until the pillars were removed. Planet had turned out a million dollars worth of copper in its fifty-four year life span.

Swansea, the other major copper camp in the Lower Colorade River region, was not far from Planet, being only seven miles directly southeast. Like the Planet, its operators were plagued by financial worries throughout most of its years.

The discoverer of the mines around Swansea has been long since forgotten. There was a legend in the district that the first miners were German. Some said that when the Clara Consolidated Company took over the claims in 1908, they discovered an old German ore car in one of the diggings.

Howland Bancroft, an historian who wrote a book about the mines of Northern Yuma County in 1911, didn't believe the tale. He found a miner who said that he had worked in the district back in the 1880s. The old-timer, J. W. Johnson, thought the ore car had been left by Americans working at that time.

Hardly anything is known about those early efforts to mine the copper around Swansea. Signal Mine must have been the most important of the early day claims. It already had six shafts when serious mining started in 1909. One was down three hundred feet.

Swansea came to life when a group of visionary promoters headed by George Mitchell formed the Clara Consolidated Gold and Copper Company in 1908. Whether by accident or design is uncertain, but they discovered to their delight that European investors, particularly those located in France, Holland, and Belgium, were eager to buy their stock offerings. Several million shares were sold, and the American promoters began making big plans.

The town of Swansea got its name from the fact that the earlier miners had once shipped ore from the Signal Mine to Swansea, Wales, for smelting. The Clara Company began building a seven hundred ton smelter[9] and purchased the old Mudersback Mine eight miles south of Bouse to provide a silver sulphide flux that would be needed in the furnace.

Transportation had always been a major handicap at Planet, but the Swansea promoters overcame that problem with the thousands of dollars from stock sales in Europe. They built a railroad, the Arizona and Swansea, which carried the product of the mines to Bouse on the Santa Fe Railroad, twenty-two miles away.

It looked for a time as if Clara Consolidated was really going to make money, and stock shot up from $ .75 a share to $22.50. But the ore was never of the high grade type that had come from the Planet. When the bottom fell out of the copper market in 1911, bankruptcy followed.

A howl went up from the overseas investors when Clara Consolidated's demise was announced, and they took over the assets of the firm hoping to salvage some of their loss. They formed a new concern, the Swansea Consolidated Gold and Copper Mining Company, and hired a French mining engineer, Camille Clerc, to serve as general manager. Though Clerc soon had the firm's two hundred and twenty-five employees turning out two hundred tons of ore a day, he still could not run the mines profitably, and they were closed down.

[9]Howland Bancroft, *Reconnaissance of the Ore Deposits of Northern Yuma County* (Washington: Government Printing Office, 1911), pp. 59-60.

A placer mining machine being set up near Quartzsite. The inventor fled to Argentina when it failed to yield the promised profits.
(1905.)

—*Courtesy Yuma County Historical Society.*

Ernest Lane, a mine foreman at Swansea, organized the unemployed miners after the closure in 1913. They agreed to work without pay until the mines became profitable. When copper prices began rising again as a result of the First World War, they received their wages and continued working as employees of the bankruptcy court.

The creditors had been paid off by 1916, and the mines were leased to Charles Clark, who was a major stockholder in the United Verde Mines at Jerome. Clark formed the Swansea Lease Company which operated the mines until 1925. Several other lessees operated the mines until the Great Depression struck in the Thirties, and Swansea became a ghost town.

As a town, Swansea was not the wild place that Hedges or Silent had been. The newspapers record very few shooting incidents, and it must have been fairly quiet. It had a newspaper, the *Swansea Times*, which was edited by Mrs. Angela Hammer. The railroad link with the Santa Fe gave its citizens a feeling of not being too remote from the civilized world.

A writer for *Desert Magazine* visited the old town in 1941 and wrote a description that conjures up some feelings of what it must have been like living there:

"From a distance Swansea had the appearance of being a prosperous operating mining camp," wrote Hilton in the January issue of the magazine. "The first building on the left was an adobe structure that had been the railroad station. Behind it was the wreckage of an old passenger coach and the cab of a locomotive that had been robbed for scrap iron. An interesting object was a gasoline-driven car with a canopy top that looked for all the world like an old surrey on railroad wheels. What a picture it must have made, chugging along the cactus-studded hills, loaded down with passengers bound for the bright lights and excitement of Bouse!"[10]

[10]John Hilton, "Specimens From an Old Mine Dump," *Desert Magazine*, IV, 7 (January 1941), pp. 13-16.

King of Arizona Mill, date unknown.

—*Courtesy Yuma County Historical Society.*

Chapter Thirteen

THE KING WAS THE BIG ONE

KING OF ARIZONA MINE produced more gold than any other single mine in the Lower Colorado Basin. Before it was closed down in 1910, it had turned out nearly four million dollars in precious metals. Though the mines around Picacho had a higher total, it was from a number of different mines rather than one.

Charles Edward Eichelberger was the discoverer. He had a reputation for being a pretty fair prospector when Epes Randolph, Superintendent for the Southern Pacific Railroad, hired him to prospect on a fifty-fifty basis in 1895. Eichelberger went out and looked for some likely ledges, but had to return to Yuma without finding anything. When he approached Randolph about replenishing his supplies, the railroad superintendent put him off. Charley waited for a time, but when it looked as if Randolph was uninterested in continuing their partnershp, he asked Henry Gleason to grubstake him. Gleason, an engineer for the Yuma Light and Water Company, was willing.

Another prospector, Charlie Carmen, was thinking about combing the S.H. Mountains northeast of Yuma. Someone had made a small strike there, late in 1894, that hadn't amounted to much, but there was a possibility that there were some larger veins waiting discovery.[1] Eichelberger decided to accompany him.

The boys followed the route of the Southern Pacific as far as Mohawk, and then struck out north for the mountains. Na-

---

[1]William G. Keiser, "Cornishmen and Chinese Cooks," *Calico Print*, IX, 3 (May 1953), p. 41.

tives of the region claim they were named the S.H. Mountains because they resemble an outhouse, but the Phoenix *Herald* said their real name was the "Short Horn" Mountains back in 1897.

Near the canyon where Eichelberger found the King, they ran out of water. The prospectors decided to separate. "I was going to that big mountain up above, where there were tanks," Carmen recalled. "Eichelberger was to come over in two days if he didn't find water, and I was to go over in two days if I didn't find water. If there was none at either place, we were going on up to Squaw Peak."[2]

Eichelberger climbed up into the canyon and found a tank with some water in it. He was fatigued by his efforts. After drinking from the tank and filling his canteen, he sat down in the shade of a desert tree to rest. Looking out across the canyon, he spied a shallow cave about twenty feet from where he was sitting. Indans had evidently used it in the past because it was blackened with soot.

His sharp eyes spotted a flash of color radiating from the soot blackened walls. Exercising the professional curiosity of a prospector, he went over to examine it. It was gold, a vein nearly three feet wide.

Carmen waited four days for Eichelberger. When he hadn't returned by the fifth day, he went looking for him and found him in the canyon glorying in his good luck. "He'd found water," Carmen said, "and he'd found the King of Arizona in a cave where the Indians had been making fires . . . And he'd located for himself. He hadn't located me any (claims) at all."[3]

Eichelberger returned to Yuma to tell Gleason about his discovery, but found the engineer a natural skeptic. Gleason didn't believe the prospector's claims were as rich as he said they were. He told Eichelberger to go out to the King and get several burro loads of ore to be assayed. When the prospector did as asked, the ore was valued at $500 a ton. Even then Glea-

[2] E. B. Hart, "First Days at the King," *Calico Print,* IX, 3 (May 1953), p. 32.
[3] Keiser, *op. cit.,* p. 41.

son insisted upon seeing the mine himself so that he could be assured he wasn't being victimized by some sort of a mining swindle.

The *Sentinel* noted that when Eichelberger went out to the King to get ore for Gleason to assay, a number of the town loafers were planning to follow him. The newspaper thought Eichelberger had slipped out of town too early in the morning for the boys, but it was wrong.[4] Two men, Cain and O'Brien, did trail him, and staked claims all over the canyon. Some of them overlapped his, and it took a lawsuit to finally straighten the matter out. A judge ruled in favor of Eichelberger's claims in every instance.

The big strike had not been unnoticed by Randolph, who staked Eichelberger originally. He had a written contract with the prospector which promised him a half share in anything Charley discovered, and it still had several months to run. Even though Gleason had grubstaked Eichelberger, Randolph thought that he was entitled to a part interest in the mine. When the railroad superintendent threatened a lawsuit to get his fair share, Eichelberger and Gleason wisely gave him a fourth interest.

It was necessary to buy a stamp mill and do a certain amount of preliminary work to get mining started, but none of the three had enough capital for that purpose. In order to acquire funds, they sold shares in the mine to the Mayor of Yuma, R. J. Duncan, and Eugene Ives, a prominent attorney with political ambitions. The five made it official by forming the King of Arizona Mining and Milling Company. Gleason was dispatched to Los Angeles to purchase a five stamp mill.

There was no water at the King, and the milling process required a great deal. The company installed the mill at Norton's Ranch, five miles from Mohawk, where there was a plentiful supply of water from the Gila River. It was ready for operation by mid-summer, 1897, and the first ore exceeded expectations. It was so rich that the mill had to be stopped

[4]*Arizona Sentinel*, Feb. 19, 1897.

Price's Saloon at Kofa, 1898.

—Courtesy Yuma County Historical Society.

every few hours to remove the gold from the plates so that it wouldn't fall off and be lost. Twelve hundred dollars worth of gold were extracted from the first two tons.[5]

The sale to Ives and Duncan gave Eichelberger and Gleason the first cash proceeds from their mine. Each received $10,000, and Eichelberger proceeded to get some enjoyment from his newly found wealth. The *Sentinel* reported that he was "setting 'em up" for the boys in the local bars, and offered the opinion that he would probably make a trip back to Pennsylvania, his state of origin.[6] The prospector fooled everyone by getting married instead. When the family was increased a year or so later by the birth of a baby girl, the proud father named the child Kofa, short for King of Arizona. Gleason sold his remaining interest in the King to Duncan and Ives. They made an offer of $100,000 which he found irresistible. Part of the proceeds were used to buy a ten acre homesite near Redlands, where he entered the real estate business and prospered.

No one was satisfied with the five stamp mill at Norton's. The company had to haul the ore thirty-five miles to get it to the mill. When it got there, the inefficient stamping process lost almost thirty dollars in gold a ton in the tailings. Though the waste problem was soon solved by the addition of 30 ton cyanide tanks, the owners were still unsatisfied because the mine was capable of producing much more ore than the mill could crush each day. A larger mill was clearly needed for the King to realize its full potential.

The ideal solution was to build a new mill at the mine, but that was impossible until there was a satisfactory water supply. As an alternative, the management discussed the possibility of enlarging the mill at Norton's Ranch and building a railroad over the thirty-five miles from the mine to the mill. When that idea was discarded as being too expensive, an aerial tramway was proposed. That suggestion was dropped too, and it was

[5]Arthur P. Thompson, "The King of Arizona Region, Yuma County," *Arizona Mining Journal*, IX, 7 (Aug. 30, 1925), p. 9.

[6]*Arizona Sentinel*, Apr. 17, 1897.

finally decided that a mill should be built near the mine if sufficient water could be found to run it.

Lack of water at the mine was a hindrance, even with the ore being milled at Norton's. Miners frequently had to be laid off because of shortages. During 1897, it was hauled from the river in barrels carried by freight wagons pulled by ten mule teams. The freighters loaded up with water, hay, and grain on the two day trip up to the mine, and carried ore on the return to the river. It was a disagreeable job that few men kept for long. "The whole road, from Mohawk to within a mile or two of the mine, had been cut so deeply by the wagons," E. B. Hart recalled, "that it was one solid cloud of dust from the time we left Mohawk . . . It was so bad we seldom rode at all. We'd get off to one side and walked. I worked only a month on the freighting job."[7]

It seemed drilling a well would be the easiest solution, but all efforts met with failure. Contractors had a well down 280 feet by October 1897, but didn't find a trace of water. Drilling continued throughout 1898, with equally negative results. When the contractors had still not struck water by January 1899, the mine cut the work force in the shafts to ten men, and the owners began to consider building a pipeline to the Gila River.

A solution came unexpectedly! Hiram Blaisdell had purchased the Venus Mine from the estate of Dr. Jayne. Shortly afterward, José Mendivil sold the old Neahr Mill at Picacho to Stephen Dorsey. Blaisdell made arrangements with the ex-senator to use the deserted mill and installed a 100 ton roller machine in the building to work Venus ore. The new machinery had only been operating a short time when the Jayne heirs suddenly brought suit against Mendivil and Dorsey. They said Mendivil had no business selling the old millsite since he had patented the land at a time he was not actually an American citizen. It began to appear that Blaisdell had installed expensive equipment on land belonging to the Jayne estate without their permission.

[7]Hart, *op. cit.*, p. 33.

Blaisdell approached the King owners with an interesting proposition. He and a partner, S. Morgan Smith, offered to form a new corporation to be known as the King of Arizona Construction Company. The new firm would move Blaisdell's mill equipment from Picacho to a location near the King and assume responsibility for finding water to run the mill. In return they asked a two-fifths interest in the King of Arizona Mining and Milling Company. Ives and Randolph accepted the offer.[8] Eichelberger and Duncan had sold their interests a few months earlier.

The deal caused legal complications that were not resolved for a decade, but it went well at first. Removing the mill from Picacho was the first hurdle. Blaisdell and Smith hired every team in Yuma to assist in transporting the four hundred tons of machinery. They found water too, though not as close to the mine as everyone would have liked. The first well was brought in fourteen miles away at Castle Dome, but drillers found a second one five miles from the mine a month later. They had to go down 1000 feet to reach it! The mill was soon running, and Blaisdell took over as general manager. He brought his former foreman, Frank Guerra, from the Venus to do the same job at the King.

Rumors were abroad by fall that the owners at the King were feuding. Substance was added to them in December when Blaisdell suddenly announced his resignation as general manager. When Guerra quit a week later, everyone knew something was brewing.[9]

A lawsuit filed in the district court at Yuma late in December by the King of Arizona Mining Company brought the dispute into the open. Named as defendants in the case were Blaisdell and Smith. Randolph and Ives charged that they had "failed to comply with the contract." They were not happy with production at the mill or in the mine. Most of the employees were of Mexican extraction and they thought they

[8]*Yuma Sun*, Jan. 27, 1899.
[9]*Ibid.*

weren't working hard enough. Ives and Randolph used the occasion of their lawsuit to announce that "only White labor will be employed at the mill and mine."[10] They hired a Cornishman, H. T. Dunne, to replace Guerra, and he gave the "Cousin Jacks" preferential treatment in hiring for years afterward.

Blaisdell seemed willing to settle the dispute out of court and move on to greener pastures, but Smith wasn't. He seized the pumping plant he had installed and asked for an injunction against the mining company. His petition to the court requested that a receiver be appointed since the company was mismanaged. It went to trial before Judge Webster Street in February 1900. Street decided in favor of Ives and Randolph and refused Smith an injunction. The judge told Smith to get off the mining company's property and to give up the pumping plant he had occupied.[11]

It seemed that the matter was settled, but it wasn't. Smith filed a new civil suit in April 1900, but lost again at a trial three weeks later. Someone lodged charges in Washington that fall alleging that Territorial Judge Street had taken a bribe from Ives and Randolph to give a favorable verdict in the Smith case. Judge Street had to go to Washington to answer the accusations. Smith steadfastly denied that he had instigated the charges, but his disclaimers must be discounted in light of his involvement. After a hearing on November 21, 1901, the Justice Department rejected the accusations as "having no foundation."[12] Shortly afterward, Smith and Blaisdell accepted a compromise settlement that was highly favorable to the King of Arizona Mining Company.

When Smith died the following year, his son, Beauchamp Smith, revived the legal controversy. He filed civil suits alleging that Blaisdell had conspired with Ives and Randolph to pressure his father into accepting an unfair compromise. He said the elder Smith was mentally incompetent at the time of

[10]*Arizona Sentinel*, Dec. 30, 1899; *Yuma Sun*, Jan. 26, 1900.
[11]*Yuma Sun*, Jan. 26, 1900; Feb. 9, 1900.
[12]*Arizona Republican*, Dec. 3, 1901.

the settlement, and asked two-fifths of the King of Arizona Mining Company as heir to the Smith estate. His suit dragged through the territorial courts for the next seven years until it was finally dismissed by the Supreme Court in 1909.[13]

The town which developed around the mine was named Kofa, a shortened version of King of Arizona. It had a hundred residents living mostly in tents by April 1897, when a stage line commenced operations which carried passengers from the mine to Tacna and the Southern Pacific Railroad for $20. An elementary school was opened in a tent for sixteen students when mill operations began to expand in 1900.

English miners from Cornwall made up a large part of Kofa's population after Blaisdell and Guerra departed in 1899. The Cornishmen (Cousin Jacks to the miners) were in great demand for mining because of their skill. Most of the supervisory crew were from Cornwall, and they gave their fellow countrymen first shot at the jobs. William Keiser, who was looking for work, was warned by Alex MacBeth, a stage driver, not to apply at Kofa.

"It's a Cousin Jack camp," MacBeth said, "and you're no Cousin Jack. You can't get a job there."

Keiser ignored the warning and went anyway. "Are you a London boy?" the Cornish foreman asked.

When Keiser admitted that he wasn't, the foreman replied, "No! I haven't got nothing."[14]

Kofa's large Cornish population may explain why it had the reputation of being a quiet mining camp. The miners brought their wives and children over from England, and they lived in the camp. The female influence may have helped preserve law and order. The old newspapers contain very few accounts of fights and killings at Kofa.

Politics played a role in the mining operations at the King. Eugene Ives, the Tucson attorney who owned much of the company stock, was an avid seeker of public office. He had no sooner established residence in Yuma County after buying into

[13]*Arizona Sentinel*, Mar. 25, 1909.
[14]Keiser, *op. cit.*, pp. 37-38.

the King, than he ran for Territorial Council in 1898, and was elected.

According to E. B. Hart, Ives hired extra personnel at the mine in 1900 so that they might be available to vote for him.

"I worked at the King through the election of 1900," Hart stated. "That was quite an election. The main interest was the re-election of Senator Ives . . . The company hired everyone they could get before the election—including a lot of Mexican laborers who had worked for the railroad. About two months before, they came streaming into Kofa to work for the company. They were all registered and they all voted. So did the Cousin Jacks. Ives won. The day after the election, they turned all the Mexicans loose."[15]

Circumstantial evidence suggests that Ives used the same stunt to win the election of 1902. R. L. Payne, a miner who said that he had been employed at Kofa, complained to the *Sentinel* that he had been fired for saying he did not intend to vote for Ives. John Dorrington, *Sentinel* editor, said that Ives "has had it advertised through the territory that there is plenty of labor at the King of Arizona."[16] Ives won the election by a narrow margin of one hundred and fifty-one votes.

Dorrington immediately accused the mine owners of tampering with the vote from Kofa precinct, which gave Ives an edge of 128-1. He said the ballot box was not delivered to the county treasurer within the time limit set by law, and that the seal on the box had been broken. Ives responded by suing Dorrington for $25,000 for libel.[17] It seems significant that Ives managed to postpone the suit each time it was slated for trial, and that he dropped it four years later.

As the mine went deeper into the earth, ore values decreased. Mining continued at the King until the summer of 1910 when ore was bringing only $2.80 a ton. The owners shut down the mine, and Kofa soon became a ghost town.

[15]Hart, *op. cit.*, p. 35.
[16]*Arizona Sentinel*, Oct. 29, 1902.
[17]*Ibid.*, Oct. 28, 1903.

Kofa is only a memory now. It was uninhabited in 1972, and would go unnoticed if it were not for a monumental tailings dump and dozens of crumbling building foundations. The mill was in ruins with only a part of the floor remaining. It had collapsed in places revealing a basement, which appeared to be too dangerous to enter. Someone had installed an iron gate over the main shaft of the mine to keep the curious from falling into it, but the gate was in great danger of being the victim of the accident it was designed to prevent.

Charley Eichelberger, the King's discoverer, suffered a fate similar to that of his mine. He was a local celebrity for a time, and purchased a home on Yuma's Orange Avenue, its version of Park Avenue. Admiring citizens elected him to the school board, and the exclusive Elk's Club accepted his membership.[18] But fame and fortune were fleeting. Part of the $140,000 he got from sale of the King vanished when a fire destroyed a laundry he had purchased in San Francisco. The remainder was expended trying to revive an old mine in the Quartzsite area, the Apache Chief. He spent $20,000 trying to interest promoters in the copper producer, but no one was willing to gamble on it.

[18]*Ibid.*, Mar. 18, 1899; Apr. 22, 1899; *Yuma Sun*, May 26, 1899.

Felix Mayhew, North Star discoverer.

—*Courtesy Yuma County Historical Society.*

CHAPTER FOURTEEN

FELIX MAYHEW AND THE NORTH STAR

HANDSOME Felix Mayhew was one of the most colorful men who inhabited the mining camps of the Lower Colorado. He wasn't much of a miner and preferred other kinds of work, but he got by better than most. Like Charley Eichelberger, he had his brief glimpse of fame and fortune. His discovery of the North Star Mine, a mile and three quarters from the King, was responsible.

Felix first turned up at Kofa in 1899, where he quickly became a well-known resident. Within the year, he was appointed deputy for Pete Burke, the mining camp law officer with the fearsome reputation. When Yuma County Democrats held their 1900 convention in Yuma, Felix was the delegate from Kofa precinct and held a proxy for four other delegates. He was able to cast five votes as the result of that bit of luck,[1] and used the opportunity to nominate himself for Justice of Peace from Kofa. He was elected in November, and had not yet been able to take office as the guardian of law and order, when he had a fight with a Mexican. The judge must have come out on the short end, since he received a broken finger in the melee.

Two other brief items related to Mayhew's affairs appeared in the newspapers before he made his big strike. The *Sentinel* reported that he had opened his "new quarters to the public on payday night," and guessed that he was "sure to do a good

[1]*Yuma Sun*, Sept. 14, 1900.

business."[2] It might be assumed he was running a bar, but the enterprise could have been some other business that was likely to attract many customers. The *Sun* carried the information that he had sold four mining claims that he owned jointly with George Norton to a Mr. S. Hall of Chicago in 1904.[3] Someone who knew him recalls that he was in the business of cutting wood for the mine by 1906, and that he owned a number of burros and was employing Mexican laborers.

How Mayhew discovered the North Star in the summer of 1906 is a matter of local controversy. The old-timers around Yuma give credit for the discovery to one of the Mexicans who worked for him, but whose name they have forgotten. They say the real discoverer did not know the value of his find, and that he showed an ore sample to Felix, who was able to locate its source, and file a claim on it.

Another version gives Felix full credit for finding the mine. One of the wells had run dry at Kofa, and he was informed by the mine management that he would have to find another source of water for his burros. He remembered a canyon north of the King where water sometimes stood in places after a rain. There had been a recent downpour, so he went there to try to get water. The rain which had fallen had washed the rocks clean and exposed an outcropping no one had seen before, even though the S.H. Mountains had been thoroughly prospected. Felix recognized the quartz ledge, and filed a claim on it.

Perhaps neither version is correct. Doubt is cast on both by the fact that when he sold his mine to capitalists six months later, he had four partners. Nick Larsen and Charles DeCorse each owned a fifth while W. D. Smith and Juan Verdugo owned twentieth shares in the claim. Mayhew still retained half of it.

The King of Arizona Mine was little more than a mile from the North Star, and its record of successful operation must have helped Mayhew sell his mine. He had no difficulty in finding

[2]*Arizona Sentinel*, Nov. 28, 1900; Dec. 5, 1900; Feb. 27, 1901.

[3]*Yuma Sun*, Feb. 12, 1904.

buyers and was able to close a deal by January 1907. The purchasers were two New York capitalists, Charles Fay and E. M. Rogers, and a pair from Denver, E. K. Humphreys and F. N. Rogers. They agreed to pay $350,000 for the mine, and then sold it to the Golden Star Mining Company for an undisclosed sum.[4]

Mayhew realized only $166,666 since he had to share the proceeds from the sale with his four partners, but it was still more money than he had ever seen. He quickly got the reputation of being a big spender. It was not unusual for him to hire a train and take all his friends to Los Angeles where he would wine and dine them in style. No one was permitted to pay for a drink in his presence. Matches were too cheap a commodity to light his cigars. $20 bills worked better![5]

A young widow, Carmelita Romero, attracted his eye and he married her. That caused problems when another lady, Mary Zabala, appeared in town and announced that she was Felix's common-law wife.[6] She said she had started living with him in 1898. The first Mrs. Mayhew said she wanted a divorce from Felix and half of the proceeds from the sale of the North Star. Felix hired Eugene Ives, the lawyer-owner of the King, to defend him. Ives didn't deny the common-law relationship, but told a judge that the statute in effect in Arizona was in conflict with federal law and therefore unconstitutional. When the presiding judge decided to take the case under advisement for a few months, Ives was able to convince the first Mrs. Mayhew that she should accept $23,500 as a balm for her injured pride. The judge was informed of the compromise and settled the matter by ruling that the common-law Mrs. Mayhew was not really married to Felix.[7] It may be presumed that all left the court room happy except Felix, who was out $23,500 plus legal costs.

[4]*Arizona Sentinel*, Jan. 16, Feb. 13, Dec. 4, 1907.

[5]William H. Westover, *Yuma Footprints* (Tucson: Arizona Pioneer's Historical Society, 1966), pp. 57-58.

[6]*Arizona Sentinel*, Oct. 9, 1907. The woman is named as "Mary Valenzuela" in an April 15, 1908 issue of the *Arizona Sentinel*.

[7]*Ibid.*, June 17, 1908.

Polaris, with North Star Mill in background. (N.D.)

—*Courtesy Yuma County Historical Society.*

That was only the beginning of Mayhew's legal difficulties. Dan Breslin sued him in January 1908, on grounds that he had helped sell the North Star, but had not had proper compensation for his efforts. He felt that $30,000 would be about right. It looked as if the dispute would be settled when it went to a jury in April 1908, but the jurors couldn't agree. Eleven of them wanted to give Breslin $500 rather than the $30,000 he asked, but the twelfth juror refused to be convinced, and the judge had to dismiss them. The case went to court a second time in December, and Breslin was granted $2,000. Another lawsuit against Mayhew was filed by the first Mrs. Mayhew's lawyer, Judge Baker, who wanted Felix to pay his legal fees. The matter was settled when Ives reached a compromise in the case.[8]

Mining had been the road to affluence, and it was natural for Mayhew to look that way again as a means of replenishing his fortune. He grubstaked two prospectors, Joe and Fred Alvarado, who found an outcropping that looked promising, the Amavisca Claim. Mayhew asserted that ore from the ledge assayed at $75 a ton. When he told the Yuma *Examiner* that he had sold part of the claim for $386,000 a few weeks later, he must have been exaggerating because the buyer was a local man, George Hodges.[9] Hodges was the son of Peter Hodges, the Kofa butcher. It seems doubtful that young Hodges had that amount of money to buy a mine.

But whatever the amount Hodges paid, he was soon feuding with Mayhew about it. When the two began quarreling in Yuma's Gandolfo Hotel on June 9, 1909, Hodges became so enraged he pulled a pocket knife and stabbed Felix twice. The wounds were minor, and Mayhew went to Los Angeles for treatment while Hodges was booked for assault.[10] Hodges was never tried, and the reason why is not clear. The explanation may be that his father, Peter B. Hodges, was murdered while

[8]*Ibid.*, Apr. 15, Nov. 18, Dec. 30, 1908.
[9]*Yuma Examiner*, Jan. 20, Feb. 18, 1909.
[10]*Arizona Sentinel*, June 10, 1909.

George was awaiting trial. The elder Hodges was lured into the desert by Francisco Marquez, who said he had a mine he wanted Hodges to see. Mayhew may have dropped the charges against Hodges in sympathy over the death of his father.

The Amavisca Mine was in the news again in July when Mayhew said that it had been sold for $300,000 to one L. J. Fontana of Los Angeles. Though the report may be true, it seems unlikely. Chances are that Fontana bonded the mine with the stipulation that he would pay $300,000 for it if it proved valuable. There is no evidence that it ever produced a single ton of ore.

Local folklore holds that Mayhew's money was gone within three years. Considering the number of lawsuits in which he was involved and the way he spent his money, it is probably right. William Westover, who wrote a local history, *Yuma Footprints*, asserted that Mayhew prospected for a new mine most of the rest of his life, but never found it.[11]

North Star Mine must have been a disappointment to its operators, the Golden Star Mining Company. It is not known how much they paid the syndicate for the property, but it must have been in excess of $500,000 because the syndicate paid $350,000 to get it from Mayhew. The owners built a fifty ton mill and began production in 1908, which produced less than $10,000 in gold that year. A fire destroyed the workings in the main shaft and threatened to trap the night crew on November 6, 1909, but the men escaped through an older shaft. It did several thousand dollars worth of damage, but the mine produced more than a half million dollars in gold that year. It produced another half million dollars in gold before closing in August 1911.[12] Golden Star stockholders only got back $140,000 of a probable investment of $750,000.[13]

[11]Westover, *op. cit.*, pp. 57-58.

[12]Dean Butler, "History of Mining in Yuma County, Arizona," *Arizona Mining Journal*, XII, 5 (July 30, 1928), p. 9; *Engineering and Mining Journal*, Aug. 11, 1911, p. 256.

[13]*Engineering and Mining Journal*, Jan. 10, 1914, p. 90.

CHAPTER FIFTEEN

THE MINOR PRODUCERS

THE LOWER COLORADO REGION has had hundreds of mines and thousands of mining claims. Many ledges that looked promising to a weatherbeaten prospector proved to be worthless when the assay reports came in. Others assayed well on the surface, but the ore body thinned out or disappeared when the miners began drilling development shafts. Some mines that people describe to winter visitors and newcomers never got beyond the development stage though the impression is given that they were important mines.

Several of the small producers have had colorful histories and deserve some mention. They are included in this chapter. Mines which produced only a few thousand dollars worth of ore have been deliberately ignored. Some minor producers may have been left out for lack of information.

BILLY MACK MINE

This old gold mine is on the Arizona side of the Colorado, eight miles northeast of Parker. It was located by William H. "Billy" Mack around 1884. T. M. Drennan, who knew Mack, said that he was working the mine by himself in 1899. "Billy is about the happiest and most independent miner I know of," Drennan told the *Sun*. He added that when Mack ran short on money, "he simply goes to his mines, takes out four or five tons of ore, runs it through his old stamp mill, and sends the bullion to Needles."

[1]*Yuma Sun*, Mar. 10, 1899.

Mack bonded the mine to some Los Angeles people in 1904 for $51,000, but they found it disappointing, and gave it up when the bond expired. The shaft was down three hundred feet by then. Bancroft found Mack running the mine himself in 1911 with his ancient five stamp mill. He guessed that the gold in the tailings was worth thousands of dollars, and estimated the old man had taken $65,000 from the mine using only hand drilling tools.[2] Information is lacking about later operations at the Billy Mack.

CINNABAR MINE

This deserted mine is ten miles southwest of Quartzsite, Arizona. Its quicksilver ore may have been first discovered by Indians. Captain Juan Mateo Manje, the military officer who escorted missionery Eusibio Kino into Arizona in 1697, found the natives using mercury in their body paints. When he asked one of them where it came from, the Indian described a mine where the Cinnabar Mine is located.

Quicksilver was eagerly sought by the early mining industry because both gold and silver readily adhere to it. Harold Weight stated in 1957 that either Mexicans or Americans discovered the Cinnabar Mine in the 1860s.[3] That may be true, but the *Sentinel* said that a French company had worked the mine for copper at that time.

How long it was mined for copper is uncertain, but it had been deserted for many years when Pete Smith of Quartzsite filed a copper claim on it in 1905. Smith showed some of the ore to Louis Judd, a Colorado mine developer and asked, "How's that for copper?"

"Damned poor copper," was the reply, "but first class cinnabar "[4]

Judd bought the claims for his Colonial Mining Company. The ore ran between five and eight per cent cinnabar at the

[2]Howland Bancroft, *Reconnaissance of Ore Deposits of Northern Yuma County* (Washington: Government Printing Office, 1911), p. 74.

[3]Harold O. Weight, "The Mine That Might Have Been," *Westways*, IL, 5 (May 1957), pp. 22-23.

[4]*Arizona Sentinel*, July 1, 1908.

three hundred foot level and contained small amounts of gold. They built a 30-ton furnace of bricks hauled in from Los Angeles and began mining. The brick furnace proved a horrible mistake. So much of the mercury was absorbed by the bricks that Colonial could barely make a profit. The firm struggled on a year or so more and gave up.

COCOPAH PLACERS

These placer diggings were on the west side of the Lower Colorado, near the east end of the Mt. Mejor Range in Old Mexico. They were discovered by Geronimo Elizaldo in 1892 and created a small gold rush. Forty men were working the diggings in 1894, but profits were not great. Eugene Corrado and three companions were reported to be averaging $50 a week.

Three American investors lost their lives when they went to examine the Cocopah Placers in 1892. Two were brothers, S. J. and C. W. Breedlove of San Diego. The other man was an easterner, Farnum Fish of Meadville, Pennsylvania. The trio had visited the diggings and promised to buy them from Elizaldo, but became lost on the return trip to Jacumba, California. The July heat and a lack of water killed all three just a short distance from a water supply.

Elizaldo said he had discovered the ledge, which was the source of the placer gold on Mayo Mountain in 1896, but his mine never became a producer.[5]

MARIQUITA MINE

There may be no other small mine on the Lower Colorado with as romantic a past as the Mariquita. It is located five miles west of Quartzsite in the Dome Rock Mountains.

Miners had placered the foothills of the Dome Rock Range for years when Jacque Travis discovered the Mariquita in the late 1880s. Travis was a Frenchman, who was barely making his living in the gulches along the Dome Rock Range using a

[5]*Arizona Sentinel*, May 7, Aug. 6, 1892; Feb. 10, 1894; Feb. 15, 1896.

dry washer that he carried on his back. He got lucky one day and found the lode from which his placer gold was coming.

Travis had very little money, so he worked the Mariquita alone. The first load of ore that he transported to a Colorado River mill netted him $4,000. The proceeds were used to finance a trip to San Francisco, where he met and married Mrs. Travis. The newlyweds returned to their Arizona mine hoping to secure enough gold to return to France and live in comfort. Less than a week after their return to the Mariquita, Travis was bitten by a rattlesnake and died. His wife walked to Quartzsite for assistance in burying him. Afterward, she barricaded the mine and moved to Chicago.

A French engineer became interested in the Mariquita in the early Nineties and journeyed to Chicago to try to effect a deal. When he asked Mrs. Travis how much she would take for her mine, the widow replied, "Two hundred and fifty thousand dollars cash!"

Falco, the engineer, answered that he could not pay that much without first having an opportunity to examine it. When he offered her $20,000 for a sixty day option to buy, she refused and the deal fell through.[6]

Mrs. Travis did accept an option of $67,000 for her mine in March 1900. Two mine operators who gave her the money told a court that she refused to turn the property over to them when they tried to exercise their option. They sued for $85,000.

The damage suit was dropped as the result of an agreement with Stephen Dorsey when he bonded the Mariquita for $100,000 in 1902. When the bond expired in December of the same year, he failed to exercise his right to buy the mine. Another operator, W. H. Alvord, made a deal with Mrs. Travis a few years later. He paid off her mortgage, back taxes, and built a stamp mill on the site in return for a half interest. The widow went to court in 1905 asking that a receiver be ap-

[6]Charles M. Clark, "The Story of the Mariquita Gold Mine," *Arizona Mining Journal*, VIII, 13 (Dec. 1, 1924), p. 9. Clark calls the discoverer of the mine Travaise, but newspapers of the period used the spelling in the text.

pointed for Alvord, and that she be awarded $25,000 in damages. Alvord filed a counter claim asking $40,000 on grounds that Mrs. Travis promised $33 a ton ore when the mine actually produced $4 a ton. He got only sympathy from a judge who ruled in favor of the widow.[7]

Production figures from the Mariquita are not available.

MESQUITE PLACERS

These diggings were located seven miles from Glamis Station in the foothills of California's Chocolate Mountains. Some unknown miner discovered the placer gold in 1880, and by January 1881 one hundred and fifty miners were dry washing in the area. Two of them, Powers and Hoagland, took out $350 in gold in a few day's time, but that was not common. Average returns ran from $2 to $20 a day. Miners considered them exhausted by 1885, and they were abandoned.

A drop in mining activity occurred as a result of the Depression of 1893, and out-of-work men remembered the Mesquite Placers. One hundred and forty Mexican miners dry washed them in the winter of 1893. Placering continued on for several more years, but began to tail off in the late Nineties. Mesquite Camp could count a population of eight men, two cats, two mules, and a burro in 1897.[8]

PAYMASTER MINE

This mine has already been mentioned in connection with the activities of Hiram Blaisdell who operated other mines at Cargo Muchacho, Picacho, and Kofa. Its history is really an episode in the story of the Poor Man's Mining District, fifty miles north of Yuma in San Diego County, California.

The Poor Man District was discovered accidentally by Mexican miners who were returning from the mountains to the Colorado River in 1876. While waiting on a lagging companion, one of them broke a piece of rock from a ledge and discovered galena, silver-lead ore. He returned to Yuma,

[7]*Arizona Sentinel*, May 21, 1902; Oct. 16, 1907.
[8]*Yuma Sun*, Aug. 20, 1897.

where he informed José Maria Redondo, who filed a claim on the Luz Vein and put several men to work mining it. Other prospectors rushed in and filed claims.

Interest died quickly owing to its distance from civilization and a lack of transportation. Most claims lapsed except for Redondo's, which his heirs maintained with the assistance of John Dorrington, *Sentinel* editor.[9] When the Silver District boom began in 1879 north of Yuma, interest was rekindled, and the district revived. Paymaster Mine was located by Howard H. Douglas, and it was the only one of the many promising claims ever brought into production.

Douglas sold the Paymaster to Lloyd Tevis and Hiram Blaisdell for $20,000 in 1885, and they built a fifteen stamp mill and started production, with Blaisdell as general manager. It produced silver until it was exhausted in 1889.

PLOMOSA PLACERS

These old diggings can be explored six miles east southeast of Quartzsite. They are three miles south of Interstate Highway 10 in the foothills of the Plomosas.

Though one source dates these diggings back to 1872,[10] they were not worked extensively until 1880, when a firm known as the Arizona Concentration Company leased 3,000 acres and began dry washing. They used expensive machines called Stephens Dry Concentrators, and worked a crew of seventy. Dr. C. M. Seeley was president of the firm, which claimed it was getting a dollar a ton from the gravel. Four machines were in operation, which could process five tons of gravel an hour.[11]

The operation lasted about a year, and production figures are not available.

SHEEP TANK MINE

The remote Little Horn Mountains, nineteen miles northeast of the King of Arizona Mine, are the location of this silver and gold producer. It was discovered in 1909 by J. G. Wetterhall,

[9]*Arizona Sentinel*, Aug. 6, 1881.
[10]*Ibid.*, July 2, 1892.
[11]*Ibid.*, Nov. 20, 1880.

but couldn't be mined until 1929 because of a lack of transportation and water. Sheep Tank Mining Company drilled a well three and a half miles south of the mine at that time and installed a 100-ton cyanamid mill. It produced nearly $200,000 worth of ore in the next few years, with silver predominating. The mine was closed in 1934.[12]

VALENZUELLA COPPER MINE

Not much is known about this copper producer, which is seven miles due north of the Dome Rock Interchange on Interstate Highway 10, east of Ehrenberg. Colonel Richard Darling bought the mine in 1901 and set a twenty man crew to work preparing it for production. They built a smelter at Salome in 1906,[13] and produced some copper. Specific production figures are lacking.

* * * * *

The mining era had virtually ended with the closing of the North Star in 1910. Agriculture has been the mainstay of the Lower Colorado's economy ever since.

Sentinel editor John Dorrington was first to recognize the change that was coming. The Algodones Land Claim Cases had been settled by 1905, and land to the south and west of Yuma had been thrown open for settlement. Laguna Dam was being built to make extensive irrigation possible. In a lengthy editorial entitled "Hen Beats Gold Mining," the editor pointed out that eggs and poultry earned the United States $280,000,000 the year before, but gold mining had yielded only $272,000,000. "Let's turn our attention to agriculture," Dorrington suggested. "The mining era is over."[14]

He was strangely prophetic.

[12]E. D. Wilson, J. B. Cunningham, and G. M. Butler, *Arizona Lode Gold Mines and Gold Mining* (Tucson: University of Arizona Press, 1934), p. 144; Charles H. Dunning and Edward Peplow, Jr., *Silver From Spanish Missions to Space Age Missiles* (Pasadena: Hicks Publishing Corporation, 1966), pp. 111-112.

[13]*Arizona Sentinel*, Sept. 4, 1901; Feb. 7, 1906.

[14]*Ibid.*, Sept. 20, 1905.

BIBLIOGRAPHY

UNPUBLISHED MATERIAL

Jaeger, Louis J. F. *Diary*. Special Collections, University of Arizona Library, Tucson.

Winsor, Mulford. "José Maria Redondo." Unpublished manuscript in the files of Yuma County Historical Society, Yuma, Arizona.

Yuma County Recorder's Office (Arizona). *Book of Deeds, Castle Dome: 1864-1865*.

Yuma County Recorder's Office (Arizona). *Book of Mines, Castle Dome: 1871-1875*.

Yuma County Recorder's Office (Arizona). *La Paz Miscellaneous Records, November 10, 1862-July 1, 1863*.

Yuma County Recorder's Office (Arizona). *Mining Claims: Book A, Castle Dome District, La Paz: December 8, 1862-October 8, 1863*.

BOOKS

Altshuler, Constance W. (ed.) *Latest From Arizona: The Hesperian Letters, 1859-1861*. Tucson: Arizona Pioneer's Historical Society, 1969.

Bolton, Herbert E. (ed.). *Spanish Explorations in the Southwest: 1542-1706*. Charles Scribner's Sons, 1930.

Browne, J. Ross. *Adventures in Apache Country*. New York: Harper and Brothers, 1970.

Dunning, Charles H. and Peplow, Edward (Jr.). *Rocks to Riches*. Pasadena: Hicks Publishing Company, 1966.

Dunning, Charles H. and Peplow, Edward (Jr.). *Silver: From Spanish Missions to Space Age Missiles*. Pasadena: Hicks Publishing Company, 1966.

Faulk, Odie B. *Arizona: A Short History*. Norman: University of Oklahoma Press, 1970.

Flint, Timothy (ed.). *The Personal Narrative of James O. Pattie of Kentucky*. Chicago: Lakeside Press, 1930.

Harpending, Asbury. *The Great Diamond Hoax and Other Stirring Incidents in the Life of Asbury Harpending.* Norman: University of Oklahoma Press, 1958.

Hinton, Richard J. *1000 Old Arizona Mines.* Toyahille, Texas: Frontier Book Company, 1962.

Murbarger, Nell. *Ghosts of the Adobe Walls.* Los Angeles: Westernlore Press, 1964.

Spence, Clark C. *British Investments and the American Mining Frontier: 1860-1901.* Ithaca: Cornell University Press, 1958.

Wagoner, Jay J. *Arizona Territory, 1863-1912: A Political History.* Tucson: University of Arizona Press, 1970.

Westover, William. *Yuma Footprints.* Tucson: Arizona Pioneer's Historical Society, 1966.

Wilson, Eldred D. and Others. *Arizona Lead and Zinc Deposits.* Tucson: University of Arizona Press, 1951.

Wilson, Eldred D., Cunningham, J. B., and Butler, G. M. *Arizona Lode Gold Mines and Gold Mining.* Tucson: University of Arizona Press, 1934.

Wilson, Eldred D., Fansett, G. G., Johnson, C. H., and Roseveare, G. H. *Gold Placers and Placering in Arizona.* Tucson: University of Arizona Press, 1961.

Wilson, Eldred D. *Geology and Mineral Deposits of Southern Yuma County, Arizona.* Tucson: University of Arizona Press, 1933.

Young, Otis E. (Jr.). *How They Dug the Gold.* Tucson: Arizona Pioneer's Historical Society, 1967.

Young, Otis E. (Jr.). *Western Mining.* Norman: University of Oklahoma Press, 1970.

NEWSPAPERS AND MAGAZINES, GENERAL REFERENCES

Alta California (San Francisco), 1860-1864.

Arizona Sentinel (Yuma), 1872-1911.

Daily Miner (Prescott), 1879-1880.

Engineering and Mining Journal, 1881-1910.

Evening Bulletin (San Francisco), 1864-1865.

Mining and Scientific Press, 1863-1900.

New York Times, 1901.

Oasis, The (Nogales), 1893.

San Diego Union, 1875.

Weekly Arizonian (Tubac), 1859.

Yuma Examiner, 1909.

Yuma Sun, 1897-1911.

NEWSPAPERS, MAGAZINES, AND JOURNALS, SPECIFIC REFERENCES

Barney, James M. "Arizona's Trail of Gold, Part I," *The Sheriff,* VIII, 2 (February 1949), 4.

Barney, James M. "Arizona's Trail of Gold, Part III," *The Sheriff,* VIII, 4 (April 1949), 9-10, 20-22.

Barney, James M. "La Paz, A Famous Placer Camp on the Lower Colorado River," *Arizona Highways,* (July 1939), 15-17.

Blair, Gerry. "From the Red Cloud—Red Crystals of Wulfenite," *Arizona Days and Ways Magazine: The Arizona Republic,* November 14, 1965, 46.

Blake, William P. "Mining in Arizona," *Arizona and Its Resources,* (August 1899), 55-57.

Butler, Dean G. "History of Mining in Yuma County, Arizona," *Arizona Mining Journal,* XII, 5 (July 30, 1928), 8.

Clark, Charles M. "The Story of the Mariquita Gold Mine," *Arizona Mining Journal,* VIII, 13 (December 1, 1924), 9.

Clark, Charles M. "Workings of Pre-historic Mines," *Arizona Mining Journal,* IX, 2 (June 15, 1925), 26.

Fireman, Bert M. "Fremont's Arizona Adventure," *The American West,* I, 1 (Winter 1964), 8-19.

Hart, E. B. "First Days at the King," *Calico Print,* IX, 3 (May 1953), 32-36.

Hilton, John W. "Nuggets to Bullets at Castle Dome," *Desert Magazine,* VII, 12 (October 1944), 5-9.

Hilton, John W. "Specimens of an Old Mine Dump," *Desert Magazine,* IV, 7 (January 1941), 13-16.

"History of a Once Famous Arizona Gold Mine," *Engineering and Mining Journal,* February 17, 1912, 372.

Hunter, A. and Henderson, R. "Boom Days in Old La Paz," *Desert Magazine,* XXI, 9 (September 1958), 19-21.

Keiser, William G. "Cornishmen and Chinese Cooks," *Calico Print,* IX, 3 (May 1953), 37-41.

McKenney, J. Wilson. "Gold Builds a Road," *Desert Magazine,* I, 2 (December 1937), 8-9.

McKenney, J. Wilson. "Saga of Old Picacho," *Desert Magazine,* II, 9 (March 1939), 10-13.

Mendivil, Mike. "Gold, Guns and Fiestas in Old Picacho," *Calico Print,* VII, 4 (February 1952), 4-7.

Minhinnick, H. J. "Some Bonanza Mines of Yuma County," *Progressive Arizona,* II, 3 (March 1926), 25.

Parker, John L. "Lost Lode Legends Plentiful in the State," *The Arizona Republic,* November 12, 1961, 14.

Ransom, Jay Ellis. "Harquahala Bonanza," *Desert Magazine*, XVI, 2 (May 1953), 16.

Raymer, R. G. "Early Copper Mining in Arizona," *Pacific Historical Review*, IV, 2 (1935), 127.

Riggs, John L. "Old Traditions of the Lost Mines of the West," *Arizona Mining Journal*, VII, 4 (July 15, 1923), 33.

Rochester, Ed. "Blame the Gold or the Climate—We Can't Get Away From Picacho," *Calico Print*, VII, 4 (February 1952), 4-7.

Thompson, Arthur P. "The King of Arizona Region, Yuma County," *Arizona Mining Journal*, IX, 7 (August 30, 1925), 9-10, 60-62.

Townsend, Clara F. "Post Office, Cafe, Boarding House, and Store— Picacho Kept Mother Busy," *Calico Print*, VII, 4 (February 1952), 4-7.

Weight, Harold and Lucille. "Tumco—Two Time Ghost Camp of the Cargo Muchachos," *Calico Print*, VII, 2 (February 1951), 4.

Weight, Lucille and Harold. "Arizona's Lost French Miners," *Westways*, XLII, 2 (February 1950), 2-3.

Weight, Harold O. "The Mine That Might Have Been," *Westways*, IL, 5 (May 1957), 22-23.

Willson, Roscoe. "Slabs of Gold As Big As a Man's Hand," *Arizona Days and Ways Magazine: The Arizona Republic*, October 25, 1964, 34-35.

INDEX

Lost Box Canyon Mine, 131
Lost Cabin Mine, 132, 133
Lost Frenchman Mine, 125-128
Lost Squaw Group, 131
Lost Squaw Mine, 129-131
Luce, Eliza, 53, 55
Luce, Robert, 55
Luce, William, 53, 55
Luz Vein, 180
Lyle, W. S., 101
Lynx Creek, 44

MacBeth, Alex, 166
MacCleod, Don, 95, 96
MacCleod, Taylor, 65, 66, 84, 95, 96
Mack, William H. (Billy), 175, 176
Madre Claims (Mine), 111
Mammoth (Claim, Lode), 40
Manje, Juan Mateo, Captain, 176
Manzonal Mine, 18
Maria de Oro Vein, 63
Mariquita Mine, 177-179
Markham, H. H., 122
Marquez, Francisco, 174
Martin, Ancil, 110
Martinez, Juan, 89
Martin, J. B., 110
Mastin, R. F., 41
Matilda Mining Company, 151
Mayes, Ed, 49, 51
Mayhew, Carmelita (Romero), 146
Mayhew, Felix, 169-171, 173, 174
Maynard, Professor, 91
McCarroll, 131
McCasey, John, 83, 84, 128
McCormick, Richard, 29
McLean, Allen, 116
Mendivil, José Maria, 57, 58, 63, 66, 73, 95, 162
Mendivil, Mike, 57, 66, 70
Mesquite Plocers, 179
Mexicans, 103, 105-107, 129, 132, 170; miner's union, 117; Lost Frenchmen's Mine, 126, 127; railroad strike, 141; Ives exploits, 163, 164, 166
Mexico, 13
Mexico City, 14
Middle Camp Mountain, 33, 34
Millar, Walter, 47, 49, 87, 88
Miller, William P., 44-46
Mineral Hill Mine, 150
Mining and Scientific Press, 17, 23, 44, 59, 79, 87, 90, 97, 102, 105, 150, 151
Mitchell, George, 153
Moberly, Missouri, 23, 25
Mohave Indians, 15
Mohawk Pass, 126
Mohawk Station, 83, 157, 159, 162
Molina, Abram, 51
Monts, Hiram, 25
Morales, 29
Moreland, 122
Moreland, L. C., 79, 80
Morgan, Samuel, 65
Mudd, Seeley W., 121
Mudersback Mine, 153
Muir, Francis, 106, 107
Mulachy, 117
Mullins, George S., 116
Murphy, W. O., 102

Nagle, George, 45
Neahr, David, 59, 61, 66, 67
New Mexico, 20
New York Daily Times, 19, 20
New York Tribune, 29
Nock, George, 38
Nogales, 4
North Star Mine, 169-171, 173, 174, 181
Northwest Leasing and Development Co., 152
Norton, George, 87, 126, 127, 170
Norton's Landing, 88, 89
Norton's Ranch, 159, 161, 162
Nugent, M. J., 23

Ogilby, E. R., 112
Ogilby Station, 95
Olive City, 33
Oro Mining and Milling Company, 98
Oroville, 21
Ortiz, 29
Osuna, Jesus, 89

Pacheco, 57
Pacific City, 89
Pacific Exchange Saloon, 95
Pacific Mine, 87, 89
Padre Claim, 111
Parker, John, 14, 15
Parks, S. S., 77
Partridge, N. H., 151, 152
Pasadena Mine, 121
Pattie, James O., 15
Paymaster Mine, 112, 115, 179, 180
Payne, R. L., 167
Pearce, Giles, 84, 85
Pease, O. A., 77, 78
Pease, Solomon, 78
Pettigrew, Richard, 67, 69
Picacho, California, 57-59, 61, 63, 65-67, 77, 80, 95, 143, 157, 162, 179; placer mining at, 57, 58; vein discovery at, 58; Dorsey at, 61, 67; high grading at, 63, 65; end of, 73, 74; English placer mining at, 79, 80; removal of mill from, 163, 164.
Picacho Gold Mining Company, 65, 67, 79
Pickenback, Charles, 94, 102, 107, 110
Pima Indian Tribe, 90, 97
Pinal County, Arizona, 51
Planchas de Plata, 14
Planet Mine, 149-153
Planet Mining Company, 149
Plomosa Placers, 180
Plumosa Mountains, 14
Pocahontas Mine (Lola), 46, 51
Poindexter, 58
Pointer, E. C., 26
Polhamus, Isaac, 34, 73
Pool (Recorder), 137, 139
Poor Man's Mining District, 179
Porter, Judge DeForest, 76
Poston, Charles, 33
Potter, A. S., 24, 25
Prescott, Arizona, 13, 90
Prescott Courier, 130
Prescott Miner, 150
Punta Del Cobre Mine, 151
Purdom, Hez, 26

Love, Frank, 1926–
    Mining camps and ghost towns; a history of mining in
Arizona and California along the lower Colorado. Los
Angeles, Westernlore Press, 1974.

    192 p.   illus.   22 cm.   (Great West and Indian series, v. 42)
$7.95

    Bibliography: p. 183–186.

    1. Mines and mineral resources—Arizona—History.   2. Mines and
mineral resources—California—History.   I. Title.   II. Series.

299362   TN24.A6L63   917.91'71'034   73-86960
           ISBN 0-87026-081-6   MARC

        Library of Congress   74 [4]